Librarian in Search of a Publisher:

How to Get Published

by Brian Alley and Jennifer Cargill

Illustrations by Barbara G. Scheibling

ORYX PRESS
1986

The rare Arabian Oryx is believed to have inspired the myth of the unicorn. This desert antelope became virtually extinct in the early 1960s. At that time several groups of international conservationists arranged to have 9 animals sent to the Phoenix Zoo to be the nucleus of a captive breeding herd. Today the Oryx population is over 400, and herds have been returned to reserves in Israel, Jordan, and Oman.

Published by The Oryx Press
2214 North Central at Encanto
Phoenix, AZ 85004-1483

Published simultaneously in Canada

Printed and Bound in the United States of America

∞ The paper used in this publication meets the minimum requirements of American National Standard for Information Science—Permanence of Paper for Printed Library Materials, ANSI Z39.48, 1984.

Library of Congress Cataloging-in-Publication Data

Alley, Brian.
    Librarian in search of a publisher.

    Bibliography: p.
    Includes index.
    1. Library science—Authorship.   2. Information science—Authorship.   3. Library science literature—Publishing.   4. Information science literature—Publishing.   5. Bibliography—Methodology.   I. Cargill, Jennifer S.   II. Title.
    Z669.7.A39   1986   808'.02   85-45512
    ISBN 0-89774-150-1

Table of Contents

Acknowledgements

The authors are grateful to their colleagues and publisher who provided information, related anecdotes, and rendered support during the writing of this book. We particularly thank Phyllis Steckler, our publisher, and Susan Slesinger and Jan Krygier, our editors, for their support and patience.

Special thanks go to John Merriman, B. H. Blackwell, Ltd., and David P. Woodworth, School of Library and Information Science, Technical College, Loughborough, England, for their helpful advice and encouragement.

Part I
So You Want to Be
a Librarian Who
Publishes

Introduction

How many times have you listened to a colleague complain about the quality of the professional library literature, bemoaning the fact that issues of primary importance were simply not being addressed clearly, thoroughly, or perhaps at all. The two of you may have observed that either one of you could have done a better job of presenting the facts in a given article or monograph or presentation and that it was a shame that information science professionals didn't make a greater effort to improve their communication skills. Either you or your colleague may have considered acting on your observations and may have even gone as far as drafting a letter to an editor before forgetting entirely about the topic of your conversation and going on to pursue more pressing interests.

We've all had similar experiences and, while some of us have accepted the challenge by making our own contributions to the literature, most of us have not. Why is this? One reason is that not everybody has something important to say or possesses the kind of skills that will ensure a successful, written presentation. For those who do have something to say and the means to say it effectively, there are numerous barriers, both real and imagined, that have a way of snuffing out that creative urge before it has time to bear fruit. Procrastination, apathy, lethargy, and all the other acquired personal traits we may recognize privately, yet hate to admit even to our closest friends, are roadblocks that must be overcome. Family commitments, social schedules, and even the requirements of an employer all make demands on our time and can, if we let them, determine whether or not we will be able to allocate a sufficient number of hours to devote to a writing project. Fear of rejection and concerns about shaky writing skills constitute real hindrances for a number of us and, until resolved, actually prevent us from committing a single word to paper.

There are scores of other reasons why we hesitate to write, but for now, it is sufficient to understand that such hazards to successful navigation through the mine fields of information science writing do indeed exist and that, in the chapters that follow, we not only intend to identify them, but also to present solutions, alternatives, and suggestions which will help the would-be author cope with them successfully. Whether we are talking about speaking or publishing an article or book, each has its foundation in the writing process. The more skill employed in the writing process, the more successful the writer will be in communicating ideas and concepts.

Conversations similar to the one we described at the beginning of this introduction have taken place regarding conference presentations, workshops, seminars, and other situations in which communication seems to be the basic need that we have difficulty resolving satisfactorily. For most of us, there is always room for improving communication skills, and that improvement can lead directly to a number of important benefits: better jobs, professional recognition, awards, and a whole group of satisfying, gratifying achievements that enhance our chances for professional progress and growth.

Considering the variety of activities connected with the information science field, there is considerable room for improvement in the quality of our current literature and lots of opportunities for new authors to make significant contributions. In the periodical area alone there are dozens of publications addressing our varied professional interests and requiring a steady flow of manuscripts in order to meet their publication deadlines. There are the more scholarly journals like *College and Research Libraries, Library Quarterly, Library Trends,* and *The Journal of Academic Librarianship,* all of which appeal to library educators, academic and public librarians, and a wide range of research-oriented professionals. Although their scope may be narrowly focused and their format restrictive, their editors are always looking for authors with a fresh approach, new topics, and significant research findings to present to their readers.

The general interest journals such as *American Libraries, Library Journal,* and *Wilson Library Bulletin* present a less formal, journalistic format. They represent the *Time* and *Newsweek* of the library and information science field and offer the potential author a variety of topics on which to write as well as sometimes giving a modest remuneration for the author's effort.

In addition, there are more narrowly focused journals such as *Serials Review, School Library Journal, Technical Services Quarterly, Technicalities,* and *Horn Book* which, though restricted in subject scope, offer many opportunities for the creative use of writing skills for professionals whose interests are closely allied with those of the publication.

Add to these periodicals the almost unlimited array of newsletters, including organization and society publications, and the potential number of sources for your writing efforts grows substantially. Around 63,000 periodical titles of all kinds are currently being published. All of the various professional organizations publish newsletters of one kind or another and, although an article in a newsletter may not support your bid for tenure in an academic institution, it may enhance your visibility in the profession and will certainly help you perfect your writing skills. Also, because the newsletter editor is always looking for material, there simply isn't a publication better suited to the needs of the beginning writer than the newsletter.

There is another category of potential publication sources well-suited to the beginner: the house organ. Commercial firms, libraries, churches, and a host of organizations publish internal newsletters directed primarily at their employees or a specific group of clients. For example, you may have already made a number of contributions to your employer's publication, but never thought much of it. However, whatever the subject matter, whatever you contribute still constitutes writing, and the house organ is a good medium in which to practice your writing skills. In many respects, any chance to write is worthy of consideration for the new author.

Obviously, there are more opportunities to get published in periodicals than in any other format. The demand for articles is relatively steady, and the chances of finding both a significant topic and willing publisher are relatively good. In this book, we will be exploring publishing in periodicals simply because of the considerable potential they hold for writers. We will also examine monographs, but with the understanding that, although you probably won't tackle a book-length manuscript as your very first project, you may decide to do that after you've had a few successes with shorter writing projects.

Choosing a topic for a monograph is similar to choosing one for a periodical article, but the competition among authors increases sharply for a monograph. There are the scholarly and professional monographs or idea books that are very narrow in scope and, consequently, limited in appeal and sales. Reference and bibliography monographs, comprising another distinct group, are appealing to both publishers and, depending on the titles selected for publication, to the public as well. Of even greater appeal is the "how-to" book which is oriented to the practitioner who needs to acquire specific skills or wants to learn new techniques. Books on library history and library education also have significant potential for the author even though they may be limited in terms of appeal outside of the profession.

Within this book, we are also going to talk about a number of other topics either related directly to publishing or related to professional activities that lead to personal recognition, visibility within the profession, and career advancement. These subjects are all intertwined and emphasis placed on one will often help promote another.

Visibility in the profession is a good example. We are assuming it is important in terms of career advancement. The attention you receive for your various achievements can and usually does lead increasingly to more and more opportunities. Those opportunities, in turn, increase your visibility and so it goes.

Every time you appear in a workshop, serve on a committee, address a gathering, present a paper, or conduct a seminar, you receive recognition from your peers. The degree of success you attain in these activities is directly related to the skill and preparation you put into them. The better you perform, the more you will be called upon to repeat your performances. There are numerous ways to improve the chances for success and to gain greater recognition. They include the speaking and committee activities we've mentioned and a host of writing assignments—writing assignments that can be turned into speaking engagements and oral presentations that can be revised and published. Presenting ideas in a variety of formats and doing it all effectively is one of the basic themes of this book.

Our reason for writing this book is not merely to acquaint you with the fact that there are publishing possibilities for new authors in the library and information science field. That's something you probably already know. What we intend to do is to provide you with reasons for improving your communications skills (primarily writing) and to encourage and motivate you by offering a variety of avenues by which you may achieve your goals. There are a number of communications objectives that individual information science professionals may have, and we intend to address as many of them as possible. The "publish or perish" threat is one obvious concern that many of us must face regularly. Others may see professional writing strictly in terms of career advancement. Then there are those who are selflessly motivated simply to making a contribution to the professional literature. Personal enjoyment experienced through writing and speaking is yet another reason for learning to improve written and oral communication skills, perhaps the most satisfying reason in the long run.

We recognize that there is a great deal of interest in writing and publishing and that information science professionals are right up at the top of the list of interested parties. If you don't believe that statement, attend the next writers' workshop in your area. You'll find an attentive audience eagerly seeking practical information and proven techniques. But there is an even greater need for *motivating* would-be writers. They already have the determination to succeed; if they didn't, they wouldn't pay money to sit through several hours of lecture and instruction. What they need is inspiration and encouragement. Motivating would-be authors is another one of our objectives. As writers, editors, and librarians, we recognize the need for motivation, positive reinforcement, encouragement, and reward. We intend to offer some or all four through examples of techniques and methods that others have used successfully. In the process of offering our suggestions and strategies, we will also offer practical ideas designed to help you assess the market for your writing, conduct a self-assessment of your own potential, learn how to fit your writing and speaking objectives into your career goals, and then offer you practical advice for building your writing and speaking skills and improving your self-confidence.

In the pages that follow, please keep in mind that there are no absolute avenues to success and that what works well for one person may not work at all for the next. If you follow the four Ps for successful writers—

PERUSE the literature to analyze and evaluate the market for your writing,
PRACTICE your writing and communication skills every chance you get, and
PERSIST with submissions—you will
PROGRESS as a writer.

In the chapters that follow, we will be covering "Getting Your Act Together": starting off, dealing with deadlines, managing your time effectively, and learning the logistics involved in getting started. Next comes "The Mechanics of Writing" with comments on the tools of the trade: typewriter, word processor, style manuals. "Writing and Publishing Book, Periodical, and Other Reviews" tackles the topic of beginning with small projects. Then we'll expand to "Writing and Publishing Articles," covering scholarly and journalistic periodicals and including choosing a topic and making contacts with editors. Next we'll examine "Compiling and Publishing Bibliographies," which includes advice on using online databases and microcomputer software for bibliography production.

"Writing and Publishing a Book" discusses such subjects as choosing a topic; proposal design; selecting a publisher; collaboration; contracts, copyright, royalties, and the business aspects of authorship; and writing and producing the final product. Indexing, graphics, and special effects; establishing rapport with your publisher and editor; marketing; and self-publishing conclude the chapter.

The next chapters are "Editing Newsletters and Periodicals," followed by "Writing for Presentation." Following is the final chapter, "Establishing Your Reputation"; the appendix contains "Sample Author Guidelines" from various library publications and a bibliography of supplementary titles.

Throughout the text, you'll find lots of personal opinion, and frequently you may find yourself in disagreement with one point or another. In offering ideas, suggestions, and techniques, we realize that not everyone will agree with our approach. However, we believe that, by being selective, the beginning writer will find sufficient material in the areas of motivation and practical advice to provide support for a successful beginning as a writer. Getting started is the hardest part, and that's where we hope we can be of greatest assistance.

Getting Your Act Together

Now that you've decided to begin a writing career, even on a modest scale, you've got to make an even more serious decision regarding the amount of time you can spare for your creative venture. You've got a full-time job to start with, family and friends and lots of time-consuming activities related to them, professional, personal, and social activities—all of which produce demands on your free time. How are you going to be able to carve out a block of time to allow you to pursue this new activity? Deciding to do it is the easy part. Backing up that decision with commitment and follow-through is quite another. If you don't want to disappoint yourself, you'll need to plan your moves carefully to make certain that you create the right environment for successful writing.

Learning to use your time wisely is probably going to be the biggest obstacle for you to overcome. You'll have to recognize immediately that you may not be able to overcome the time problem completely and that, throughout your writing career, you'll have to do battle with it constantly. Even those who write full-time have problems devoting their attention to their avocation simply because there are so many other activities demanding their time.

If you are not already an expert at managing your time, you will want to seriously consider looking for a time management workshop or seminar and signing up. They are held frequently in or around most urban centers and often in conjunction with continuing education programs at colleges and universities. A time management workshop conducted by a skilled instructor can tremendously affect the way you deal with your waking hours. Practicing some of the tenets of time management won't give you any new time to devote to your projects, but you can see how to analyze your current activities and eliminate the unnecessary and wasteful ones. Then you'll be able to start reallocating that time to writing.

While you are attending the time management workshop, you'll also be receiving valuable tips and suggestions for managing your time in other aspects of your life, including your regular job. Most time management workshops are excellent, productive experiences. Some, unfortunately, are not. Don't give up if you run across a bad workshop. The next workshop will, in all probability, give you just what you want.

While scouting for a time management workshop in your area, be on the lookout for a writing seminar. Once again, colleges and universities are obvious places to look, along with community continuing education programs. *Writer's Digest* sponsors a series of writing seminars, usually one day in length, in larger metropolitan areas where they are certain to attract a large audience. Although their emphasis is usually on writing for the commercial market, they are eminently practical and loaded with helpful methods which come from years of proven experience. Their seminar leaders are successful writers who have a wealth of knowledge and are delighted to share it with the audience. Not only do they dispense quantities of helpful hints but also large doses of enthusiasm and motivation, both of which you can use as you get started and again months or even years later if your interest wanes and you need a psychological lift to get moving again.

Another popular periodical for writers, appropriately called *The Writer,* regularly lists upcoming writing seminars and workshops taking place around the country, many of which are held during the summer months. If one is scheduled for your area, seriously consider attending. There are also local writing groups that sponsor workshops. If all else fails, contact the English department of the nearest college and find out what's being offered in the way of writing courses. If you don't want to take the course for credit, consider auditing it. The experience is bound to produce benefits, both practical and motivational.

SCHEDULING THE TIME TO WRITE

Your job-related responsibilities are always going to impinge on your writing schedule to some extent, and since that is what keeps bread on the table and the proverbial wolf from the door, you'll have to consider how your new writing avocation is going to affect it. If your principle occupation takes place in an academic setting, part of your employment contract may identify specific allocations of release time for research purposes. Of course, having that prerequisite included in your employment contract can also produce a negative effect, that of considerable pressure to produce.

If release time for research purposes is not part of your employment agreement, you are going to have to find ways to create blocks of time to use for writing purposes during off hours. Are you, for example, willing to use vacation time to write? Can you organize your time so you can actually set aside an hour or two a day just to write? There is often time at the beginning or end of the day that you can put to good use. Whether or not that approach is successful will depend to a large degree on your personal lifestyle and whether or not you can do something as creative as writing in short time periods. Some people simply can't settle down to work unless they feel there is plenty of time to get mentally organized and into the right mood; many writers freely admit that it takes a total of three hours to produce 45 minutes' worth of productive effort. To find out what your capabilities are, you are going to have to experiment and establish some time sequences that seem to work best for you.

There are the morning people and the night owls, plus a few of us who fall in between or for whom time of day has no appreciable bearing on the ability to be creative. If taking the early-morning approach won't work at home, try arriving early at your work place and putting in the writing time before colleagues arrive. You can use the same technique at the end of the work day by staying an extra hour a day a couple of times a week. However, let your coworkers know why you are there or you'll be dubbed a workaholic and treated as a threat to the stability of the work place. Also remember that your regular work is going to be there to nag you silently while you write, and its presence may become distracting. If you can overlook the pile of work on your desk while you are laboring on your personal project, so much the better, but if you can't, you'll have to seek out a different environment.

Are you willing to spend a certain amount of each weekend on research and writing? Can you schedule those necessary weekend chores in such a way that you'll find sufficient time to do some serious writing? Can you actually keep the weekend chores from becoming an excuse not to write? If the major stores and shopping centers in your area of the country are closed on Sundays, the time after church or the time devoted to methodically plodding through the Sunday paper may be ideal for writing. If you can force yourself from being distracted by the new movie at the neighborhood theater, the old movie on channel 19, or the football game on cable, you are well on the way to success as a writer.

Depending upon the kind of relationship you have with yourself, you might want to consider getting into the habit of promising yourself a disgusting personal indulgence as a reward for devoting large chunks of time to writing. It could mean the difference between feeling horribly guilty at having put off the writing project for the umpteenth time or being smug and self-satisfied at having gotten chapter five written in record time. We'll leave the selection of the "disgusting personal indulgence" up to you, but don't participate in any until you can honestly say you've fulfilled all of the terms and conditions of your personal contract. You'll find you can be a pretty hard taskmaster and that the rewards can actually be satisfying even though it all takes place as a personal game between you and your alter ego. This form of carrot-and-stick self-deception need not become a regular component of your writing career, but if you need the encouragement of a reward system to get you motivated to the point of producing on a regular schedule, give it a try.

If all this talk of schedules and time management is getting you down, don't become discouraged. It is necessary to lay the groundwork, to build a writing framework within which you can reasonably be expected to produce some worthwhile creations. Hit-or-miss writing—grabbing the time when you can—simply won't work. It is frustrating and leaves you too many opportunities to come up with excuses for procrastination. By establishing a regular work schedule, you guarantee yourself the time you need. Without it, you won't ever be able to fully test your real writing skills.

What about your responsibilities to your family and friends? They may feel, and rightfully so, that you should have a sense of commitment that requires you to spend a certain amount of your time with them. It is going to be up to you to acquaint them with your new project and its importance to you and to let them know that you need time—"release time"—to devote to it. If they understand how enthusiastic and determined you are, they are bound to cooperate. After all, everyone needs time to pursue personal activities. Children can be taught to understand that parents need time to pursue their own interests. Adults may have a harder time understanding, but if you make it clear that your mental well-being or your professional future can be enhanced by your writing projects, they should be willing to cooperate. Once you've had a few successes, they'll be convinced of the value of your new endeavors and will actually suggest ways for you to find more time to write.

However, you are going to have to devise your own set of persuasive methods for making convincing arguments since you know your relatives and friends better than anybody else. You are going to have to be firm in explaining your schedule to the people who need to know. No backing down once you make the announcement! Let them know you are serious. They have to understand that the extra hours at the office or the blocks of time you set aside in the evenings or on weekends are vital to your success and don't qualify for casual chats, frequent interruptions, or other impromptu diversions. Setting up your work schedule and making it stick may be the most difficult part of your new avocation. Once the spouse, child, friend, lover, or live-in gets the idea that writing is truly important to you and that you need the time alone to satisfy your determination to be creative, s/he will be more likely to cooperate and support your work.

Depending on your own personal set of circumstances, you may have a more difficult time convincing the significant other of your need. Perhaps s/he requires a little more assurance that you will still be available, especially if your past record suggests a tendency toward failure to follow through on commitments and promises. To counteract any signs of doubt, you may want to plan for time with, as well as time away from, those who are being requested to support your writing schedules. If you proceed carefully, you just might be able to plan an all-round better allocation of your time for all concerned. Be prepared to live up to your promises, however. There's nothing worse than unwittingly creating the feeling that you are trying to get away from obligations and commitments, using writing as an excuse.

What about yourself? Knowing that you've got the schedule arranged and a green light to go ahead with your writing does not mean that the task ahead is going to be an easy one. If you want to improve your chances for success, you'll also have to prepare yourself mentally and emotionally for the task ahead. You must be able to make a reasonably long-term commitment to this new enterprise of yours. A good way to start is to identify a dozen or more goals or objectives which you can reasonably expect to achieve as a result of writing. Here are a few questions you can ask yourself to examine your own motivations.

Will the writing lead to:

- personal recognition?
- a promotion, a raise, or both?
- a more secure job?
- beating out a professional rival?
- satisfying a personal need—the need to succeed?
- recreational satisfaction, release from boring work routines, or a diversion from uninteresting or nonproductive activities?
- professional recognition?
- consulting or speaking opportunities?
- new skills that could be part of a retirement activity?

- working with leaders in your profession?
- successful promotion of your organization?

There are many other goals you can identify, ones which will more closely fit your own particular set of circumstances.

So far, our emphasis has been placed on addressing the need to set aside time to write and on establishing a regular writing schedule. But can it ever be abandoned? Is it going to be something that will run on and on without end? Must everything else be ignored while you concentrate on your writing? The answer is both "yes" and "no." On the one hand, you'll have to be fairly rigid about adhering to any schedule or you won't accomplish a thing. However, putting your schedule aside temporarily is inevitable. The trick is in not losing the momentum you've so carefully established when you find that you must interrupt your work schedule. If you've got to take a family outing, attend a conference, or meet some other commitment, work out a trade-off. If you are about to give up your writing day this weekend, insist on spending twice the time on your next scheduled writing weekend. If you can't follow your before- or after-work writing schedule on a particular day, identify lunch hours or some other time period when you can make up that lost time.

You must also establish a calendar for completing certain projects. For example, when will you expect to have a certain percentage of your research completed? When will you have the first draft of an article done? When will you have the first draft of a chapter completed so that you can have your coauthor or an objective colleague review it and make suggestions? Not establishing a calendar will lead to trouble for you *and* those who work with you. And don't just make a schedule and expect to follow it slavishly. You won't. Note your schedule on your work calendar where you will see regular reminders of your writing commitments. The saying "out of sight, out of mind" really applies here. You must constantly expose yourself to your writing schedule. Noting self-imposed deadlines on your office calendar provides you with the equivalent of a "tickler" file for your avocation.

GOAL-SETTING AND DEADLINES

We've discussed identifying the benefits you hope to receive from your writing. You should also identify your writing goal. Do you plan to complete an article? A conference presentation? A book? At the end of a year, do you want to be able to have that first article in print in the journal of your choice? By this time next year, do you want to have your book manuscript in the mail to the publisher?

Set some reasonable goals on a daily, weekly, monthly, and yearly basis. To determine what's "reasonable" for you will take a little time spent in the self-assessment process. If you know your limitations, keep them in mind when you devise your goals. The goals must be attainable for you personally. In a day, you might expect to have a certain number of words or pages written. In a week, you might have a portion of an article, presentation, or book drafted. Think in terms of drafts and revisions. In a month, you might have a second draft written and revised. In a year, you might be working on the galleys of a completed book manuscript. You know your own work pace best. Be honest with yourself and establish a realistic time frame for your goals. On a first project, you may want to establish very limited, easily achieved goals. That way you won't be disappointed too soon and you will begin with a certain sense of accomplishment. You're not going to be able to finish an article in a day, but you might finish a very rough draft in a couple of days—the sort of rough draft that gets your basic ideas on paper so you can flesh them out later.

Establishing reasonable deadlines frees you from the guilt you tend to feel when you fail to meet unrealistic deadlines. If you do miss a deadline, analyze the reasons behind the failure. Why didn't you perform up to your own expectations? If you really do not feel you can set your own deadlines, have a colleague who is knowledgeable about you and the task you've set for yourself establish the deadlines for you. By the time you begin your next project, you should be able to establish them yourself.

Adhere to deadlines as rigidly as possible. By missing them, you will become discouraged and run the risk of damaging the positive mental and emotional attitudes you have established.

TIME MANAGEMENT

What is time management? Obviously, it has to do with planning your time so your tasks are performed efficiently and effectively. Plan those tasks so that you can accomplish what is necessary. Don't let yourself look for ways to avoid writing. Don't feel you can't write unless you have your favorite pen or have found that perfect article supporting your thesis. That's called procrastination and is a pitfall to avoid.

Tips on Time Management

- List in advance what you expect to accomplish in a particular writing session.
- Have your writing tools and materials readily available so you don't waste time searching for them.
- Don't use two different mechanisms to complete your writing assignment for that session. For example, don't draft in longhand with the expectation of eventually keyboarding the

work you've completed. Learn to draft at the typewriter or
word processor and print out what you have completed so
you can revise easily. Then plan to make your revisions at
the beginning of the next session.
- Don't allow clutter to dominate your work space. Put away
unnecessary things. File what needs to be filed. If you are a
hoarder, learn to throw away extraneous materials. Learn to
do it now. Don't put it off until later.
- Turn off the phone or turn on the phone answering machine,
if you have one, and learn to ignore this common source of
interruptions. Ignore the door as well. Practice the art of
withdrawing from your surroundings while you write.
- Don't shuffle paper. Deal with each document and proceed
from there. If you can't complete a task now, set a time when
you will and then adhere to that commitment.

This is a good place to elaborate on time management and its
nemesis, procrastination. Perhaps the most important aspect of time
management is recognizing that it is your time and that not only
must you avoid wasting it, but you must also prevent others from
wasting it for you. Without being so obvious as to be labeled
"manipulative," you should try to find ways to organize the time of
those around you, simply in order to improve the chances for successful management of your own time. The parent who organizes the
children into particular play routines has at least the promise of a
certain amount of free time to devote to his/her own project. With
the kids, you may be able to get away with being a flagrant manipula-
tor. With another adult, you'll want to proceed with caution and plan
subtle moves that accomplish your objectives without being obvious.
To paraphrase the golden rule in this instance, you'll be doing unto
others before they do unto you.

Organize your work space. Establish simple, regular routines. Use
simple scheduling and planning techniques. Identify what needs to be
done by defining the tasks you hope to accomplish. Make lists of
things you want to do. You have limited time to devote to this new
avocation, so you must plan in advance to manage your time effectively. Create an agenda of what you need and want to do. Establish
both short- and long-term objectives and check them off when they
are completed. Organizing, planning, and writing down objectives
may all seem unnecessarily bureaucratic, but unless you are willing to
make this investment up front, achieving your writing goals may be
impossible.

One technique to help you identify blocks of time is to keep a
diary of how you spend your time. Review the diary and you'll
quickly see which activities account for wasted time. Did you repeat-
edly spend time looking for something in the clutter of your office?
Did you make numerous, unproductive phone calls? Did you make a
trip to a store when a phone call could have saved steps? Did you

stop what you were doing to talk with someone about the relative merits of a new book? Once you have studied the diary, you can design a plan that will begin to provide you with more time. Be determined to cut out your time-wasting activities. Where are there brief unused blocks of time when you can accomplish those short-term tasks? What tasks did you impose on yourself that could have been assigned to someone else or for which you might have hired someone who could do them for you? Periodically monitor how you use your time to see if you have fallen back into those old time-wasting habits.

As you analyze your free time and your occupied time, you may find that many tasks that require your attention can be done by others whom you can hire. Decide whether or not you are willing to hire someone to clean house, type, mow the lawn, or repair plumbing in order to allow you blocks of time for writing and research.

But don't overdo it! If you dwell on the time factor too much, you can create unnecessary stress for yourself. Keep in mind how you accomplished what it was you wanted to do in other personal or job-related situations. How did you find the time to complete those tasks satisfactorily? Reviewing those particular situations may help you now in finding the time to write. Narrowing the focus of your general expectations can be done by setting goals and deadlines. Using the pressure of time will help speed up the process.

Look at how long it takes you to complete a given task. Avoid the temptation to spend too much time and energy on a single task. We tend to spend too much time and effort on trivial matters that do nothing to help us reach our goals. Perform only those tasks which need to be done. You know which ones they are. Don't waste your time on something just because it is familiar or you like to do it. Practice self-discipline.

The antithesis of good time management is procrastination. One way to avoid procrastination is to deal with tasks and complete them when they need to be done rather than promising yourself that you will do them tomorrow. Putting off the job because you don't like it will not get it completed and out of the way. Go ahead and tackle it and then get on to those more rewarding and goal-oriented tasks.

Procrastination can also take the form of spending large amounts of time on tasks that don't really lead to achievement of a goal. An example of this pitfall would be spending a major portion of your free time attempting to produce a perfect photocopy of an article, even going so far as to copy both sides of the sheet, when the result, an article, is going to be read and later discarded. Spending time and energy on perfectionist photocopying allows you to avoid other tasks, ones that would mean progress toward a valued goal. Procrastinators are often perfectionists who utilize their penchant for perfection to avoid other activities.

Depending on your individual personality and personal work habits, eliminating procrastination can take considerable self-discipline and will require both a positive attitude and the willingness to establish goals and objectives. If you are willing to admit your tendency toward procrastination and enlist the help of friends and colleagues, they will remind you when you are about to fall into procrastination's trap. Procrastination has to be exposed and recognized before it can be treated.

There are many articles and books that will help you with time management. Most discuss the concept from the viewpoint of the business world. However, even the business-oriented texts can be helpful to someone who is interested in using time management skills to achieve personal goals. Following this chapter are a few citations to books and articles that may provide valuable insight into your own time management problems.

LOGISTICS

The Office: Your Private Work Space

Be willing to take the time to organize your private work space. Providing a comfortable, efficiently organized work space is an essential element for successful writing. Set aside a place in a spare room or even in a corner of a room that will be identified as your office. Don't let it become the repository for the photographs from your vacation or a place to stash miscellaneous other items until you have time to store them. View the area as your office in the same manner in which you approach the work area at your regular nine-to-five office.

But before we go too far, let's stop and consider. How do you view your formal job office? Is it cluttered and disorganized? If so, then your home office is likely to be the same. Do you subscribe to the "cluttered desk theory"? Remember a basic concept of time management: An effective manager has a clean desk. You will waste time if your time is consumed by the need to wade through piles of papers on your desk in order to get to the work at hand.

Have important names, addresses, and phone numbers handy so you don't have to search for them. Invest in a file cabinet or file boxes and then make sure you use them. Don't promise yourself that you will file that document tomorrow. File it now and then go on to the next item of business on your work session agenda. And put those files to additional use by organizing future work sessions before you quit for the day. Know what you accomplished today and what you want to accomplish tomorrow. Keep a file of "things to do" and be conscientious about working your way through that file. Being able to see what you've completed and knowing what the next step is will help you realize your goals sooner, with far less time wasted. And do it all with a positive, progressive attitude.

In setting up your files, do not allow yourself to keep trivial, superfluous materials or data. If it is unlikely you will ever want to look at a particular item again, don't squirrel it away. Discard it. Keep a record of the particular citation if you wish but don't keep the hard copy. That's what libraries are for.

Don't clutter your files with unneeded duplicates of letters or old, outdated correspondence. If you've finished with materials that are no longer relevant, don't play archivist. You probably don't have the storage space to spare in the first place and you certainly don't have any free time to spend on unproductive activities like sorting, stacking, and cataloging.

Set up the office so you are not easily distracted by people or objects or activities; bookcases make great room dividers. Be willing to close the door and insist on your privacy. Don't let yourself become a self-interrupter. Have all work aids and information at hand so you don't have to stop what you are doing to go get a ribbon or a tablet or a book.

The Equipment

The subject of equipment will be dealt with in more detail in Chapter 3, "The Mechanics of Writing." However, a part of getting your act together and practicing effective time management involves having appropriate equipment. By that, we mean being prepared to invest in a good electric typewriter or, if your resources will allow it, a microcomputer complete with word processing software. By now we assume you are committed to writing and are willing to invest in your commitment. Having the right tools for the job is essential.

Spend time accumulating suitable pens or pencils, decent quality paper, typing stands, and copy paper holders. Try to assemble quality writing tools before you begin your writing. Having them on hand in anticipation of needs will eliminate the frustration and bother that go with the jerry-built, make-do approach.

Beginning Your Writing

Once you have decided that you want to write, have convinced the people in your life that you are serious about it, have identified the blocks of time necessary for this avocation, and have set up your work space, how do you begin? Somewhere along the line, you should have been thinking of where you wanted to begin this writing career. In case you haven't, you should know that you have several options.

Book and Periodical Reviews

There are numerous book and periodical reviewing opportunities. Book reviews are comparatively brief and, depending upon the publication, may vary from general overviews to in-depth evaluations. Beginning your avocation by writing reviews is often merely a matter of volunteering and then submitting a sample review for consideration (there may be a trial period during which your work is critiqued). Agreeing to write reviews not only requires that you read and evaluate the materials offered but that you adhere to deadlines; it is imperative that new materials be reviewed as quickly as possible. Procrastination will eliminate you from the ranks of reviewers quickly. As a start, however, reviewing is hard to beat. You will quickly learn to meet those deadlines and your writing will become clear, concise, and to the point.

Reports

Writing reports on conferences attended or continuing education opportunities for your organization or for a publication is another way to begin a writing career. Again, timeliness is essential, so you must be able to meet deadlines consistently and prepare coherent accounts of your observations. Your regular job organization may require that in order to attend a conference or a continuing education session, you write a report on it. If it isn't required, volunteering to prepare such a report for publication could be the next step. When you volunteer for something, it is your idea and consequently it becomes a more pleasant task. When you are required to do it, the assignment can become a chore, and your creative effort suffers.

Other types of reports that you might write would be product analyses, grant proposals, procedural reports, budget proposals, and activity reports. The ability to make accurate observations and then to put those observations into a coherent report takes skill and talent that is acquired through experience. The more you write, the better your writing becomes.

Letters

Letters to colleagues are another writing medium. We all produce written correspondence, yet we don't think of it as good writing practice. It is. Extending this talent to writing "letters to the editors" presents another writing opportunity. But be sure you have something to say that expresses your opinion cogently, corrects a misconception, or voices support for a viewpoint. Most "letters to the editors" have a maximum letter length. Familiarize yourself with the rules. The briefer, more concise letters stand the best chance of being printed.

Experience with book reviews will help you reduce your letters to the salient points.

Articles

What kind of article are you interested in writing? One that is journalistic in tone? Or something scholarly, heavily researched, and footnoted? What periodicals do you prefer to read? The answers to these questions will probably help determine the type of article you will be best at writing. If you don't like to read a particular journal, then it is unlikely that the journal's style is one you can match when drafting an article for submission.

Book Chapters

Does a colleague want you to contribute a chapter to a book s/he is editing? Is the chapter needed in an area in which you have expertise? Are you interested enough in the topic to be persistent in performing the research? Is your writing style compatible to that of the other contributors? Can you meet the deadline? It is not an easy job to edit a book of chapters submitted by a variety of authors. Be sure you can meet your commitments before agreeing to be a contributor.

Papers for Presentation

Have you been asked to speak at a meeting? Have you volunteered and been accepted? Is the paper to be formal or informal? Can you write the paper in such a way that it will be both pleasant to listen to and, at the same time, informative to the audience? Keep in mind that papers written for presentation are different in style and approach from papers written for publication. After making an oral presentation, if you decide to submit the paper for publication, accept the fact that it will have to be reedited and probably largely rewritten before it will be acceptable.

Books

In many ways, it is easier and much more pleasant to write an entire book. The size is satisfying in terms of words and pages, and you don't have to cut your best prose to fit space constraints. However, you also have to have enough to say to fill a book. Or, if it is a compilation, do you have enough willing contributors of chapters to complete the book you have agreed to submit? Don't start writing the book unless you have a publisher's commitment in the form of a contract. You are apt to experience great frustration if you write a book and then go looking for a publisher. However, you should be aware that a few publishers will not issue contracts until the manuscript is complete.

Workshops, Seminars, and Classes

Putting together workshops, seminars, and classes will also test your writing abilities and build your confidence. There will be introductions and summaries to write, some of which will be written on the run so to speak. Writing for workshops, seminars, or classes will test your ability to write for a structured, formal setting with severe time constraints imposed on the length.

Brochures and Pamphlets

Often, you'll have opportunities to contribute to publicity brochures or pamphlets written to relate information about a profession, an activity, or a cause. Your writing in such instances must be succinct and clear. The finished product has to catch the eye and, at the same time, deliver a message. In the process of producing the end product, you may be working with a graphics artist, designer, and even a printer, all of whom will be involved in the production process. Once again, the discipline you experience will be a valuable asset to your writing career.

Newsletters and House Organs

Writing for a newsletter or house organ or editing such a publication is another way to pursue your interest. The topics must be timely, and the contributions should usually be short and written in a journalistic style. Such publications can lead you into a variety of writing activities.

Columns

Your local newspaper may need a weekly or monthly column related to library activities, an occasional book review, or another topic of personal interest to you. Again, you must be willing to practice self-discipline in meeting those unending deadlines and in expressing yourself clearly and concisely. Periodicals are also another potential source for publishing columns. State association or national journals change their columns periodically and may be receptive to your column ideas if they are of wide interest and fill an obvious need.

Let's Go!

Clearly there is a wide variety of formats, styles, and content to choose from in making your first attempt at writing. All of the previously mentioned forms provide good experience and will help you build skills and confidence. You'll find out just how good that variety of experience is when you eventually undertake a really difficult writing project and suddenly realize that you can draw on your valuable, hard-won skills to get the job done.

We've discussed your interest in writing; warned you about the pitfalls of procrastination, the benefits of time management, and the importance of self-discipline; cited several sources for additional information on time management; described your work space; and listed opportunities for writing. Now it's time to get started. Good luck!

SELECTED SOURCES

Atkinson, Philip. "Achieving Results through Time Management." *Management Services* (British) 28 (4) (April 1984): 28–30.
Advocates using a diary to identify how you use your time and to identify the time wasters.

Barnes, Roger T. "Time Can be on the Side of DP Managers." *Data Management* 22 (1) (January 1984): 30–31.
Shows how to allocate time effectively by delegating tasks.

Harris, Nancy N., and Sutton, Robert I. "Task Procrastination in Organizations: A Framework for Research." *Human Relations* 36 (11) (November 1983): 987–95.
Emphasizes what fosters procrastination.

"How to Forestall Interruptions that Waste your Time." *Professional Report* (January 1984): 20–21.
Discusses how to avoid self-interruptions.

Karmin, Mayanne. "Time Management and Personal Effectiveness (A Conversation with Ron Stupak)." *Bureaucrat* 10 (Winter 1981–82): 29–32.
Gives tips for managers on doing role analyses to determine how time is used.

Kiechel, Walter, III. "Beat the Clock." *Fortune* 109 (13) (June 25, 1984): 147–48.
Tells how to avoid becoming a workaholic.

Kozoll, Charles E. "Five Easy Steps Help Build Time Management Skills, Increase Efficiency." *Data Management* 22 (5) (May 1984): 18–21.

Present five steps: remembering, believing, self-directing, concentrating, and monitoring.

Lakein, Alan. *How to Get Control of Your Time and Your Life.* New York: NAL, 1974.
Perhaps the best known book on time management, this work and its author are considered the originators of the recent emphasis on time management. Provides tips on the best way to avoid wasting time.

Lampton, William. "Becoming More Productive by Closely Examining Your Day." *Fund Raising Management* 15 (2) (April 1984): 88.
Identifies ways to free up blocks of time in your day and prioritize tasks.

Rabjohns, Reginald N. "Making Your World Brighter." *Life Association News* 79 (1) (January 1984): 69–72.
Advocates practicing self-discipline and setting objectives.

Sandburg, Dorothy. "Time Management and Personal Organization." *Word Processing World* 3 (November–December 1976): 39.
Gives suggestions for planning your routines and identifying time traps.

Schmidt, Gene L. "How to Get the Most from Every Working Minute." *Executive Educator* 6 (4) (April 1984): 22–23.
Includes a time management quiz to evaluate individual work habits.

Solomon, Abby. "Organized Time." *Inc.* 6 (1) (January 1984): 123–28.
Stresses using time management software to keep track of appointments, notes, telephone numbers, phone calls; calculating; and keeping lists.

Taylor, Harold. "Encouraging Good Habits." *Computerdata* (Canadian) 8 (11) (November 1983): 20.
Explains the difference between good and old habits.

Taylor, Harold L. "Time Equals Profits." *CA Magazine* (Canadian) 117 (2) (February 1984): 74–78.
Stresses that how time is used is important, not how fast a task is completed.

Vickery, H. B., III. "Time Management: A Matter of Organization." *Association Management* 34 (12) (December 1982): Supp. A44–A45.
Gives tips on organizing yourself for effective time management.

The Mechanics of Writing

There are several aspects of the writing experience which must be considered before you actually begin to write, including choosing equipment, preparing the manuscript, handling correspondence, and keeping track of expenses and other business concerns.

EQUIPMENT

If you plan to begin your writing using pen or pencil, don't feel that the quality of your work will suffer simply because you are ignoring modern technology. Many people do their best writing by first putting pen to paper. Pen or pencil obviously provides you with mobility by allowing you to work in just about any location and under most conditions. No matter what tools you use, what is important is to begin outlining or jotting down your ideas well before you begin the actual writing process.

Dictation equipment should also not be ignored. Graham Greene used to dictate his novels on reels of tape whenever he went abroad. He would then send them back to England for transcribing. After he received the transcription, he would edit and rewrite the material. Use of dictation equipment allowed him to continue work wherever he was. He eventually got his ideas on paper and then could mold them, according to his own writing style. Today there are pocket-sized or compact recorders that use micro- or minicassettes that will operate for hours on batteries. Not only do they lend themselves to office use, but they can also serve as a valuable time-saver for you once you form the habit of dictating while traveling, while driving to a meeting, etc.

Not everybody with dictation equipment has the secretarial or typing assistance to do the necessary transcribing. But, even if you're one of those who doesn't, don't drop the idea altogether. One of the values of dictation is that you can record your ideas as quickly as they enter your mind. You've probably had the experience of having a fantastic idea and, in the process of writing it down, suddenly losing critical parts of it. By recording your ideas as they occur, directly onto tape, you are taking advantage of technology in order to improve your writing.

OK, so taping your thoughts is a time-saver, but what about the transcribing? Well, it is certainly possible to do it yourself by using a foot switch to start and stop the recorder so that you can do your own transcribing accurately and at a speed that suits you best. Because you're already familiar with what is on the tape, your transcription (assuming that you have some typing skill), will be an accurate representation of what's on the tape. It will also be "clean" in that, during the transcribing process, you will have eliminated the grammatical errors and fumbles that occur naturally in the spoken word.

If you have grown up using the typewriter as a basic writing tool, don't think you are taking the wrong approach to writing by making your original drafts directly on your typewriter. There is no "wrong" approach to the mechanics of writing. If you don't know how to type, you should certainly learn to do so simply because this is the basic skill used with both the typewriter and the word processor. If you use a typewriter, select one with a correcting feature. If you have access to an electronic model with memory, especially one with the capability to save text on diskettes, you will save yourself, or your secretary, vast amounts of time. Use of electronic typewriter memory allows you to draft your initial ideas and then revise numerous times without having to keyboard the entire text again. If you do not have access to a memory typewriter and have little hope of purchasing one, consider buying a new or well-maintained, used IBM Selectric. They have dropped in price with the advent of electronic typewriters and word processors and are a good investment for both the serious and beginning writer. You can easily find an inexpensive, reconditioned model for sale as a result of an office converting to the more modern electronic technology.

Also worth investigating are electronic typewriters. They too are the victims of an intensely competitive marketplace and as a result, continue dropping in price to the point where they can now be purchased for only a few hundred dollars. When it comes to advantages, they have a number worth considering. Most have anywhere from a line to several pages of internal memory. They have a self-correcting feature to handle your typos, offer a variety of typefaces from which to select, and are relatively trouble-free and quiet. A word of caution, however: If you decide to invest in an electronic, memory typewriter, look ahead to the day when you might decide to graduate to a microcomputer word processor and make sure your new electronic typewriter can also serve as a letter-quality microcomputer printer if attached with the proper interface. A number of electronic typewriters offer this feature and, because of the size of your investment, it is well worth exploring. If and when you do graduate to a microcomputer-based word processor, your Selectric or electronic typewriter will quickly be relegated to limited service for the typing of infrequent postcards or survey forms. If it will also double as a letter-quality printer to support your word processing system, so much the better.

Finally, the state of art in writing today is presented by our increased reliance on word processors or microcomputers with word processing software packages. If you are serious about using your time wisely, word processing will allow you to do just that. There are several excellent books on writing with computers. One such title is *Writing in the Computer Age: Word Processing Skills and Style for Every Writer* by Andrew Fluegelman and Jeremy Joan Hewes. Another author who has tackled the topic of writing with word processors is William Zinsser in his *Writing with a Word Processor.* A major ingredient of these and other books and articles is a motivational message aimed at convincing people to use word processors for writing. Peter McWilliams is another such writer, whose books *The Word Processing Book* and *The Personal Computer Book* are great confidence builders. Increasingly, the periodicals aimed toward writers emphasize the use of these modern technological wonders. The periodicals for users of microcomputers feature articles about writers who use word processing even for such specialized tasks as writing award-winning Broadway plays.

You can also use a dedicated word processor as your basic writing tool, but it is more likely that you would decide on a multiuse microcomputer with a word processing software package instead. You'll want to start off with a reliable, recognized brand, one that has local service available and, at least initially, some form of local training. There are many brands of microcomputers on the market. Our advice is to select one with a proven track record and one for which there is a variety of tested software available, with more on the way. If you will be using the microcomputer primarily for word processing, a monochrome monitor is better for long sessions of keyboarding than a color monitor. However, if you will also be using the micro a great deal for spreadsheets with graphics or other applications relying on color representations, you'll need the color monitor. Obtaining two double-sided disk drives is advised. Purchase as much internal memory as possible, keeping in mind, however, that you may want to add more later.

Today, among microcomputers, the industry standard is the IBM PC and the long list of compatibles made by other manufacturers to emulate IBM PC performance and use software designed for the IBM PC. Compatibles are offered under such brand names as Zenith, TeleVideo, Leading Edge, Compaq, Epson, Eagle, and ITT. A fully configured IBM PC with 256K of internal memory, two double-sided disk drives, and a monochrome monitor will cost $2,000–$2,500, depending on where you buy it and how many extra components are added. The compatibles follow the same general price range except that, in order to be competitive, they offer such inducements as extra memory, bundled software (free software), and special pricing incentives. If the IBM PC is the industry standard, the compatibles all attempt to meet or exceed it. In purchasing a compatible, make certain that the software you intend to use with it will actually run on the machine you've selected. There are degrees of compatibility, and it is up to you to make sure that, before making a $2,000 investment, the machine in question will really perform all of the tasks that are important to you.

Don't be misled by offers of a thousand dollars' worth of "free" software to sweeten the deal for your particular compatible. It may well be valuable software, but not if you don't find it useful. There are large numbers of microcomputer users whose bundled software gathers dust in an attic because it turned out to be something less than the software of choice when the time came to start word processing in earnest.

Did we ignore Apple, Commodore, Texas Instruments, and a host of other microcomputer manufacturers? Not at all. The bibliography at the end of this book provides sources for investigating their products. However, we feel certain that by focusing on the industry leader and compatibles, a prospective purchaser will have available a far wider range of state-of-the-art software and peripheral equipment.

Where do you purchase your word processor hardware? There are a number of national franchises such as Computerland and Entre which offer hardware, software, training, and service. They may have sales from time to time, but by and large, they sell equipment at the manufacturers' retail prices. Because they don't discount their products, they can afford to offer substantial customer support (handholding, if you will). If you need training and want the assurance of a helpful expert close by, the franchise dealer will appeal to you. At the other end of the spectrum is the mail order house, where hardware and software are heavily discounted. Most such companies accept bank charge cards, offer a toll-free number for orders, and give assistance with problems via the telephone.

In between the hometown franchise dealers and the mail order discount firms are a number of small dealers who attempt to offer personalized service locally. They offer a wide range of products, and their prices tend to fall somewhere in the middle range. Like the franchises, they will help out when things go wrong. When investigating local microcomputer dealers, also determine what kind of repair service is available.

What about printers? If most of your printing will be standard 80 column, providing formats that fit vertically on an 8½-by-11-inch sheet, look at printers with that capacity. A dot matrix printer offers considerable speed and is acceptable for most applications; keep in mind that letter-quality printers are much more expensive than dot matrix. If you intend to produce many drafts and considerable quantities of printed material, dot matrix is for you. Some of the newer dot matrix printers produce near letter-quality results and fall in the $300–$500 price range. Be sure the printer has both tractor and friction feed features so you can use either continuous feed paper or single sheets. Check the price of replacement ribbons also. Some printers use ribbons that cost as much as $15–$20 while other perfectly acceptable, reliable printers use ribbons costing $4–$8. If you find you want to be able to continue to keyboard your next chapter while the previous chapter is being printed, you'll want to acquire a micro buffer or a print spooler. Printers have limited capacity buffers built in, but for big jobs, a separate device is necessary.

An IBM PC or compatible microcomputer with two double-sided disk drives, a monochrome monitor, and a plain-vanilla, 80-column dot matrix printer can be acquired for less than $3,000. Because of competition, prices for most products are decreasing. As a result, the dot matrix printer you might have purchased in 1984 for $400 is now available for $300. As more new products appear, so do price cuts and special offers.

What about word processing software? There are literally dozens of packages offered and each claims to be just the one for your application. If you aren't familiar with word processing for microcomputers, you will find the variety of packages offered to be mind-boggling. All of the manufacturers try to convince you that their packages are truly comprehensive, yet you are going to be the judge in the final analysis—usually *after* you've made the purchase. That's the wrong time to find out that you've made a mistake.

How do you know what to select? You can and should read product reviews. They appear in a variety of sources, including the popular computer-oriented periodicals such as *Creative Computing, Byte, Personal Computing, Infoworld, PC,* and *PC World.* After you've narrowed the field somewhat through your research and reading efforts, talk with your friends and colleagues and find out what they use and why. Don't settle for the recommendation of the first person you ask. Keep asking, listening, and comparing notes. You want to identify the popular packages for your microcomputer and the one or two that sound right for you. Try to get a demonstration disk (software vendors frequently offer them for a few dollars) and take it to your local computer store and ask for a demonstration. If one of your friends has a copy of the software package, have him/her show you how it works. If professional colleagues use word processing software, find out which varieties they recommend. Do the same with educational professionals. When you eventually buy, it will be helpful to know who the local users are in case you need help. Microcomputer users' groups are another source of information. They are usually identified with a particular brand; a visit or call to a local computer store will tell you how to locate the ones in your area. You may want to join such a group if you find one that is actually application-oriented.

Microcomputer experts will often tell you that you should select your computer based on the software you intend to run. That's a great idea, but in actual practice for most of us, it doesn't work out that way. We are not that well organized and tend to buy the computer first and then one or more software packages recommended by a dealer, friends, or an absolutely overpowering product review we read in a computer magazine. Every word processing software purchase you make will cost you anywhere from $50 to $400, so the more good judgment you can bring to bear on your selection, the better. Following are some word processing software suggestions worth thinking about.

- Keep in mind which packages your employer uses. Many large companies have negotiated special purchase arrangements with software vendors for quantity purchases. Many times these special purchase agreements have provisions for employees. If you purchase a copy of the same word processing software your employer uses, you may receive it at a substantial discount and, best of all, you will have the assistance of fellow employees who are already familiar with the software and can help you get started and, later on, help you execute some particularly difficult aspect of the program.
- Keep your word processing software purchase as simple as possible so you won't be attempting the impossible with an overly complicated and difficult-to-learn-and-operate package. The authors, for example, use Volkswriter Deluxe, version 2.2, which is a menu-driven word processing package that is exceptionally easy to learn and yet handles all word processing needs. It is designed to run on the IBM PC and compatibles and is moderately priced.
- Buy your word processing software where you can get the lowest price. That usually means by mail order. The latest version of a popular word processing package is listed by the manufacturer as retailing at $295, yet it regularly sells from a popular mail order house for $159. When you fill out the

registration card for your purchase, you are entitled to any and all customer support services from the manufacturer, no matter where you bought the product. Buying software retail when you can get it for up to 50 percent off through a mail order house is a questionable practice to say the least.

- Select a compatible spelling checker to complement your word processing package. Check with friends or colleagues, read reviews, call your word processing software manufacturer, or ask to try a spelling checker at a local computer store. We use IBM's Word Proof, which easily handles files created on Volkswriter Deluxe. We don't use it so much for individual spelling weaknesses as we do for calling our attention to typing glitches we make as we're inputting. You can keyboard as fast as your fingers will go, knowing that your spelling checker program will ultimately catch most of your typos.

- Be stingy with your software dollar. Believe it or not, you won't need more than one word processing package, your basic operating system software, a spelling checker and—if you intend to dial up databases, mainframe computers, or use electronic mail—a communications software package. Beyond the basics, your software acquisitions can be left to impulse purchases and the size of your discretionary budget. The software purchases we've listed will set you up with a solid word processing capability on an IBM PC or compatible for under $400.

Don't dismiss equipment and technology as an unnecessary expense. A word processor can cut your writing time in half and improve the quality of your writing at the same time. You will probably find yourself using all of the previously mentioned tools—pen and pencil, tape recorders, typewriters, and word processors—at some point in your writing career. No matter which writing tool you select, the hardest thing is to get those first thoughts and words on paper or disk. Use whatever means are at hand that will get you to that point, whether they be "low tech," like a No. 2 pencil, or "high tech," like the word processor—whatever will help you get that first draft accomplished.

MANUSCRIPT PREPARATION

Before you begin the actual writing of your first draft, be sure to have on paper or in mind an outline of what you plan to cover. This does not have to be a formal outline; it may be nothing more than a listing of ideas with a series of subtopics. As sketchy or as informal as this outline may be, it will nevertheless provide you with a framework around which you can begin to build your writing. Be sure that the outline remains close at hand, on a bulletin board, attached to the wall, or otherwise easily visible so you can refer to it often. If you have a microcomputer, there are even specially designed outline programs such as ThinkTank, by Living Videotext, Inc., and Thor, The Thought Organizer, by Fastware, Inc., both available for use with the IBM PC and compatibles.

Once you've outlined your ideas, it's time to do that initial draft. You may find it difficult to get those first words down, but write them you must. That's where the use of dictation equipment may help you get started. Keep in mind that, while that first draft may look disastrous, the important point is that you have gotten your thoughts on paper. You may find that writing the first draft is a matter of sitting down at the keyboard and letting those thoughts flow from your mind through your fingers into reality. At this point, don't worry about spelling, format, or even organization. If you have that list of thoughts or your rough outline nearby, you can be sure that the ideas you cover will be in that order. However, concentrate your energies on excising your ideas from your mind and putting them down in black and white. Much of the first draft will disappear as you begin to revise, but the basic concepts you are trying to convey will remain. Composing this first draft is really a prewriting process, in that you are putting onto diskettes or paper what will later become your written document. If you use a microcomputer, follow these steps:

- Assign major segments of a large document on individual disks. For example, with a book, you should initially put each chapter on a separate diskette. This will enable you to take individual chapters and work on them independently, even taking the diskettes from home to work, wherever you have compatible machines available. Of course, you may have the capacity to put much more material on a single disk. However, with one major segment on each diskette, you have less to lose in the event of a catastrophe.

- Back up these diskettes regularly, certainly after each inputting session. Store the backups in a different location. Be sure to keep both copies away from magnetic fields—magnets, telephones, dictation equipment.

- If you are working with an editor and hope to submit your work on a diskette, be sure your program is acceptable to the editor (who may have specific requirements tied to the publisher's specific brand of word processing hardware).

- Print copies of your drafts regularly. A notebook is a good place to keep them. The paper copies can be carried easily for impromptu editing or revising on your part, and you can then correct the diskettes when enough changes have been made.

FIGURE 1. Proofreaders' Symbols

Symbol and Examples	Meaning
^	insert
process	insert a period
pocess	insert a letter
O.k., he said	insert punctuation
add ?/	insert?
	delete
process.	delete a period
pr~~r~~ocess	delete a letter
using ~~fountain~~ pen	delete a word
oryx Press	make upper case letter
~~D~~ictation	make lower case letter
Fourteen Grand Place	make into a number
14 people	make into a word
fountain/pen	separate
1 4 people	close up
club dinner	transpose
dinner]	move right
[dinner	move left
Grand Hotel	put into italics
~~fountain~~ pen	leave as is
¶ Using dictation	start new paragraph
no ¶ Using dictation	do not start new paragraph
Grand Hotel	make bold type

Subsequent drafts will involve tearing apart and putting back together this first draft. By the third or fourth draft, what you have written may bear no resemblance whatsoever to that initial effort. However, the first draft served an important purpose: It started your thought processes and transformed your ideas into written form. Don't hesitate to go through as many drafts as necessary. You will find that if you or your typist uses a memory typewriter or a word processor, you will be less reluctant to tackle as many drafts as necessary to get the finished product exactly the way you want it. Using a regular electric typewriter or pen and paper will restrict your writing, and you will find yourself more than a little hesitant to revise large portions of your material when you know it will have to be retyped.

The final version should be the best possible one you can put together. This is the version on which you do the final editing or the one your editor reworks with you. This edited version, whether edited by you or someone else, will possibly need additional work in order to clarify phrases, correct local colloquialisms, or otherwise improve the writing.

The copyedited version will probably be returned to you covered with proofreaders' symbols. You should be familiar with them; they appear in many style manuals and dictionaries. They are widely accepted and will provide you with a much easier way to edit manuscripts.

Style Manuals

If you are writing for a particular publication or publisher, determine what style manual they follow. This is particularly important if you are including bibliographic citations. It is also important to determine whether or not you should use arabic numbers or write out the numbers or whether you should footnote at the end of each page, at the end of the chapter, or at the end of the book. Publishers' in-house style manuals are listed in *Style Manuals of the English-Speaking World: A Guide* by John Bruce Howell (Oryx Press, 1983). This guide also lists style manuals by subject areas. You should also purchase a standard, recognized style manual for your own use. Some of the well-known manuals listed below are readily available in most bookstores.

The Chicago Manual of Style. 13th ed. Chicago: University of Chicago Press, 1982.

MLA Handbook for Writers of Research Papers, Themes, and Dissertations. 5th ed. New York: Modern Language Association, 1982.

Turabian, Kate L. *A Manual for Writers of Research Papers, Theses, and Dissertations.* 4th ed. Chicago: University of Chicago Press, 1973.

Author Guidelines

If you are writing for a periodical, ask the editor if author guidelines are available. These may be formal, printed procedures or may simply be a case of the editor asking for a particular journalistic style of writing as opposed to a scholarly one. Don't waste your time by writing a scholarly article for a journalistic publication. Ask first. There are even some periodicals, particularly at the professional state organization level, which are simply a series of columns designed to relay news to constituents. Periodicals often publish their guidelines in specific issues so check to see if the periodical for which you are writing has done so. Others do not provide formal guidelines but, nevertheless, expect clean, double-spaced, readable manuscripts to be submitted.

Correspondence

Before writing anything, whether it is a book, an article or report, or a review, consult with the editors to see if they are interested in what you plan to write. A query letter stating your idea may be sufficient for a periodical. With book publishers, you will need to present a prospectus, along with a summary of your credentials. It is important to initiate effective communication with editors or editorial boards so that you are not wasting either your time or theirs when you submit your text.

KEEPING TRACK OF EXPENSES

As you become more involved in writing, be sure you form the habit of keeping track of your expenses. Expenses related to your writing are tax-deductible. Just make sure to retain receipts for your expenses and be prepared to show that these expenses are either related to your profession (for example, you are required to publish in order to retain your position) or that your writing is an income-producing activity which you want to document with an accounting of the expenses for tax purposes.

Before you go too far, it is a good idea to consult one of the books available on taxes and expense recordkeeping for writers, such as William Atkinson's *The Writer's Tax and Recordkeeping Hand-*

book. Also, be aware of the current IRS regulations and note changes that occur during the year.

It is a good idea to open a checking account for your writing income and expenses if you find that you have the potential of receiving substantial amounts of money for your work. On this account, you should be prepared to write checks for every writing-connected expense.

You should also look for a CPA or tax preparer if you have any concerns about your ability to deal with income tax planning and filing. Among the expenses and income you will want to record are:

- Reproduction and mailing of questionnaires used in researching an article.
- Supplies, such as ribbons, diskettes, paper, film, and audiotapes, used in conjunction with your writing.
- Photocopying costs.
- Telephone charges.
- Computer software purchased expressly to use with your writing.
- Travel, if necessary, to research your topic.
- Artwork and photographic services.
- Secretarial services for typing and transcribing.
- Income from royalties.
- Honoraria for writing projects.
- Fees for writing-related activities.

THE BUSINESS SIDE OF WRITING

Before you start writing anything as substantial as a book, be sure that you have a contract and that you and the publisher have a firm agreement. There may be a possibility of doing some negotiating with your publisher, but it is likely that the negotiating will be very brief. If you have established a separate bank account, deposit those royalties for supporting further writing-related expenses. You may want to organize your writing activities as a formal business, sole proprietorship, or a Subchapter S corporation and request that royalties be paid to your business. That way you can file a separate income tax return for your business which will reflect your income and expenses from writing and identify it separately from your personal or family income. Your tax accountant or CPA can help you with further advice on this subject.

If you have a microcomputer and you need to keep detailed financial information regarding your income and expenses, you may want to consider purchasing accounting software packages which sell in the $80–$200 range and are capable of managing several individual accounts, balancing your checkbook, itemizing your expenses by month and by expense category, and furnishing a multitude of income and expense reports. Not only are such accounting software packages invaluable at tax time, but their ability to forecast and project income and expense activity and provide detailed reports on every aspect of your business gives you excellent control over every dollar you earn. Managing one of these accounting packages takes a certain amount of discipline, but that's something you'll have to have anyway if you are going to become a writer.

One popular accounting software package available for the IBM PC and compatibles is THE HOME ACCOUNTANT PLUS from Continental Software Co. (11223 S. Hindry Ave., Los Angeles, CA 90045). This package can define a minimum of 100 budget categories (more depending on the capability of your PC) and monitor transactions for cash, checkbooks, credit cards, income, expenses, and other assets and liabilities. It will keep track of items you'll want to retrieve at tax time and will search and retrieve transactions by date, check number, payee, amount, budget category, item description, or any combination of these items. It will keep track of up to five separate checkbooks, reconcile your bank statements, print reports, and even write checks. That's just a few of the things this particular package will do and yet it costs less than $100 at popular mail order software houses. Certainly, it is more of a package than you need to start off with, but as you expand your writing and as you accept consulting fees and receive remunerations for other related activities, you'll find more and more uses for your automated accounting package.

TIME TO BEGIN

Now that we have covered most of the mechanics, let's begin to tackle your writing efforts.

Part II
Writing for
Publication

Writing and Publishing Book, Periodical, and Other Reviews

As information specialists, we are all familiar with reviews of books, periodicals, media, and, increasingly, of microcomputer software. Many of us consult reviews daily in an effort to select appropriate acquisitions for our collections, to identify and evaluate reference sources, to obtain specific background information about a given title, and often, just to choose enjoyable personal reading material. Following the agenda presented in this book, we must also consider reviews in yet another light: as a potential outlet for our own writing efforts.

What do we mean? Well, maybe you have not given a thought to the process of reviewing, critiquing, or reporting on books since you were in college or graduate school and critiquing materials for collection development courses. Now is the time to revive these old reviewing skills and put them to work for a new purpose. Reviewing books is probably the easiest and yet one of the most productive ways you can find to go about launching a writing career. Consider the several magazines and journals you read or consult on a regular basis. How many of them contain reviews of books, journals, or other materials? Go through that stack of magazines beside the sofa and make a list. Mentally review the reference shelves where you work and think of those tools that you consult regularly, the ones that contain reviews of publications as well as other nonbook materials. Consider your own particular reading interests, areas of knowledge, and even hobbies. In what subject area do you have special expertise? What professional subject interests are directly related to your career, such as collection development or rare books? Do you pursue a hobby or special area of interest outside of your profession? Are there periodicals that are devoted to those interests and that contain reviews of related materials?

Identifying the types of reviews you want to write is a matter of sitting down and determining what is being published in the areas of greatest interest to you and then taking stock of your own reviewing potential. Have you had enough experience in the profession to feel confident about your ability to review new periodicals knowledgeably and objectively? Do you have time to read books or analyze reference materials, including time to spend comparing the books to related publications in the same areas? Do you know enough about nonbook materials to feel confident about comparing and analyzing what is available in other nonbook formats as well as evaluating their strengths or weaknesses compared to traditional books and periodicals? Are you sufficiently familiar with microcomputer software to be able to analyze, compare, and contrast similar programs? Do you have access to the necessary hardware to enable you to carry out the evaluations for such specialized reviews? Do you have access to other software packages that perform similar functions so you can test and compare? Software reviewing takes specialized knowledge and skill, but if you have the background and can produce readable, detailed, and accurate reviews, there is a good market for your talent.

If you decide to write reviews, begin by identifying the periodicals that contain the reviews which you read or consult on a regular basis and make a list of them. You should also consult *Ulrich's International Periodical Directory* and other, similar periodical directories that list periodicals by categories. List those periodicals in the particular subject areas of interest to you and then locate copies of them so you can see exactly what types of reviews—if any—are published. In effect, you should be making a complete analysis of each and every possible reviewing source that will fit your own special interest profile. As you compile that list, try to keep the following questions in mind:

- Is the periodical published by a society or organization?
- Is a book review editor identified?
- Are the reviews written by different individuals? (This may be difficult to determine if the reviews appear unsigned.)
- Are the reviews narratives about the contents of the book, focusing on whether or not the book is well written, or do they offer evaluative recommendations such as a "good read"?
- Are the reviews extremely analytical, making comparisons to other works?
- Are the reviews of fiction or nonfiction, monographs, or reference bibliographies?
- Are reference works or bibliographies the topics of most of the reviews?
- What is the writing style of the reviews—scholarly or journalistic?
- Do most of the reviewers seem to be "big names" or are the editors relying upon relatively unknown practitioners?

Reviews are very often the end product of committee activities. An example is the American Library Association's prestigious *Reference Books Bulletin* Editorial Board, formerly the Reference and Subscription Books Review Committee, which reviews materials individually. The draft reviews are then critiqued by other committee members before being published as a product of the committee. The published product appears unsigned though the membership of the Board is prominently indicated in each issue of *Reference Book Bulletin,* which is published within the covers of *Booklist.*

Reviews by individuals are far more common, although they may be either signed or unsigned. Until recently in the information field, the most prominent example of unsigned reviews were those appearing in *Choice,* a publication of the Association of College and Research Libraries of the American Library Association. Other publications also print unsigned reviews, reasoning that they want to keep the reviewers from being subjected to direct or indirect pressures from publishers, authors, and readers as a result of having committed their opinions to print.

Worries about reprisals aside, signed reviews are still more common. Signing the review puts the reviewer on the spot when it comes to criticism. Authors, as well as disagreeing readers, have been known to write critical letters to the publications and the reviewers with whom they disagree. The signed review not only acknowledges responsibility, it also forces the reviewer to weigh criticism carefully. The reviewer must be prepared to face contrary arguments about the opinions expressed in print. Almost every published work will elicit different responses from different reviewers, and some will be expressed more vehemently than others. The more prominent and well

known the author or the topic, the more likely it will be for the review to elicit widely differing opinions.

Before you launch your reviewing career, try writing a review of the book you just finished reading. After you have written the review, ask yourself some hard questions:

- Did you enjoy writing the review or was it a chore?
- In comparing your review to several already published in review sources, did your opinion differ greatly from those expressed in the reviews you read?
- Was your review complete in its coverage of the book or did you miss some major points?
- Did you absolutely hate the entire exercise of writing the review? If that is the case, don't proceed any further.

Contacting book review editors or committee chairs is the next step. If you are interested in reviewing for a committee, whether it is a committee that publishes its reviews or a committee such as the various notable committees that review books in order to formulate judgments for presenting awards, your first step is to identify and contact the committee chair or secretary. Ask what the rules are for reviewing materials for the committee, specifically how to become a committee member, and therefore, a reviewer. Undoubtedly, membership on the committee will be one criterion. Appointment by the association president may be necessary. In other instances, the chair of the committee may be the person making the initial membership selection, perhaps with the final appointment being made by yet another elected official. Be prepared to sell your qualifications as a reviewer and to emphasize the special qualities that make you an exceptionally good potential reviewer for the committee.

If the publication you select prints reviews by individuals, begin your inquiries by contacting the review editor, if there is one. If there is no review editor identified on the publication's masthead, address your inquiry to the editor of the periodical. Be sure to consult a recent issue to make certain that the person you contact is indeed the incumbent. In your query letter, express your interest in the periodical and make it clear that you are familiar with it. The response you receive from the editor might be one of several:

- S/he might indicate that all reviews are written by staff or by paid, professional reviewers, selected by the editor. If the latter is the case, consider filing the reply until you qualify for professional reviewer status.
- You might receive an interest inventory questionnaire to fill out and return. It is used as a means of identifying your particular areas of expertise and/or interests in reviewing books in certain subject areas.
- You might be asked to submit a sample review for evaluation.

- You might be told that only well-known authorities are asked to write reviews. Again, if you think you might someday gain that status, file the letter for future reference.

Writing a sample review in order to convince the editors that you are capable of writing reviews is a very likely requirement for the new reviewer. In anticipation of this response, you might consider submitting a sample review or two with your query letter. It is probably better, however, to wait until you are asked to send a sample review. The decision is yours and depends on how determined you are to get started. In the meantime, it would be a good idea to draft one or two reviews and keep them handy for possible submissions against the day when examples of your work are solicited.

To start thinking in terms of reviewing, take notes as you do your current leisure reading. Look at books similar to the ones you read for fun. Take a critical look at your style. Do not try to write a scholarly review of a book written in a popular style. Read reviews in the journals to which you hope to submit the sample reviews and determine how they are written. Don't adopt the exact style of their current reviewers but do note and follow the general style and format. Keep your intended audience in mind at all times.

Don't settle for the results of your first draft. Spend more time polishing and refining your review, taking considerable pains to correct spelling, punctuation, and grammar. Make the review interesting to read and, at the same time, concise and to the point. Ask a colleague to read your draft. If the colleague isn't particularly knowledgeable on the subject area, ask him/her to analyze the review, based on readability and coherence. Then, if you know someone who is acquainted with the subject, ask for a specific evaluation in terms of accuracy.

As you draft your review, do not try to emulate the style of other reviewers of the same work. Be original. You've read the work. You are now an expert and, as such, are entitled to your opinions as long as they are factual and accurate. You may even spot something of significance that the other reviewers failed to note. You may develop a completely new slant on the topic and one which potential readers will appreciate. After you have finished your sample review may be a good time to locate published reviews of the same title and compare notes. Then you can see what the other reviewers wrote and determine how your efforts measure up. If your opinions differ widely, could you still defend them? Did you miss major points? Were you constructive in your criticism? Did you draw comparisons with other comparable works? If your efforts seem to have produced good results, you now have an adequate sample ready to support your request for future reviewing opportunities.

When you send in your query letter, with or without your sample review, be sure to describe yourself to the editor by including a one-page biographical sketch. This brief narrative tells the prospective

editor who you are and how you and your interests will fit the publication's reviewing requirements. The biographical sketch can be a useful device to employ when you submit articles to periodicals, offer proposals for presentation at conferences, or make requests for appointments to professional committees. Wherever a brief summary of your educational background and professional status and activities is required, your biographical sketch will come in handy. Take special pains creating it, restrict it to one page in length, and polish and refine it with the same care and attention to detail that you would use in preparing your federal income tax returns. Be honest, be brief, and be factual. Be sure to include both work and home addresses with appropriate telephone numbers for each. Once you've produced the perfect sketch, make several equally perfect copies and keep them on file. Take a hard look at the master copy periodically and update it just as you update your longer resume or add to your list of professional accomplishments. If you have a word processor, you can store this brief biographical sketch on disk and keep it handy for frequent updating. You'll find your biographical sketch will be a great icebreaker and will serve a variety of useful purposes.

REVIEW SOURCES

In this section, we will list some key reviewing sources available within the library and information science field. This is far from being an exhaustive list; it is by no means complete. New periodicals regularly appear and old standbys may drop review sections or modify their review policies. Review editors are not always listed since they change regularly. As a potential reviewer, you should examine current issues of the periodicals in order to identify the review editor and the current style of the reviews they publish.

American Reference Books Annual (ARBA). Libraries Unlimited, P.O. Box 263, Littleton, CO 80160.

Choice. 100 Riverview Center, Middletown, CT 06457.

College and Research Libraries. Association of College and Research Libraries, American Library Association, 50 E. Huron St., Chicago, IL 60611.

Journal of Academic Librarianship. Mountainside Publishing, P.O. Box 8330, Ann Arbor, MI 48107.

Library Hi Tech. Editor: Nancy Melin, 42 Grandview Dr., Mt. Kisco, NY 10549.

Library Journal. R. R. Bowker, 205 E. 42nd St., New York, NY 10017.

Library Software Review. Book Reviews: Nancy Herther, Roman Data Systems, P.O. Box 22643, Robbinsdale, MN 55422; Software

Reviews: Nancy Melin, 42 Grandview Dr., Mt. Kisco, NY 10549.

Media Review Digest. Pierian Press, Box 1808, Ann Arbor, MI 48106.

RQ. Reference and Adult Services Division, American Library Association, 50 E. Huron St., Chicago, IL 60611.

Reference Books Bulletin. RBB, American Library Association, 50 E. Huron St., Chicago, IL 60611.

Reference Services Review. Pierian Press, P.O. Box 1808, Ann Arbor, MI 48106.

School Library Journal. R. R. Bowker, 205 E. 42nd St., New York, NY 10017.

Serials Review. Pierian Press, P.O. Box 1808, Ann Arbor, MI 48106.

Technicalities. Brian Alley, 2057 S. Glenwood Ave., Springfield, IL 62704. *Technicalities* irregularly includes a review column entitled "Worth Noting." Reviews of books and software are included.

Wilson Library Bulletin. H. W. Wilson Co., 950 University Ave., Bronx, NY 10452. WLB generally uses column editors as reviewers.

For an interesting history and discussion of procedures of some major reviewing sources, read "Reviewing the Reference Reviews" by James Rettig (*Reference Services Review* 9 [October–December 1981]: 85–102). While some of the procedures and policies of the reviewing sources mentioned have changed, the article does provide a glimpse into the way reviewing tools function.

THE REWARDS OF REVIEWING

The rewards of reviewing are many and so are the frustrations. It is a time-consuming activity and requires considerable patience, including the willingness to work over a given paragraph until it has been reduced to its simplest form while still conveying the substance of your thoughts. Remember, reviewing is not your full-time occupation and as a part-time, after-hours activity that relies on your having also devoted many hours to reading the works reviewed, you just might decide to restrict your publication efforts to reviews. It is not too hard, when reviewing for multiple publications, to suddenly end up inundated with books and/or software to review, with all the deadlines threatening to tax your available time to the limit. Reviewing could become the only writing activity in which you ever indulge—or it could be just the beginning of a whole series of other writing pursuits.

What are the rewards for all this careful, painstaking work? Name recognition is one obvious reward that comes from reviewing. You can establish your subject expertise and can become known for your opinions of the works published in that area. Getting your name recognized in the profession will lead to a number of other opportunities and offers that may be important to you. They may include invitations to contribute to reference works that are compilations of biographies of writers, requests to submit papers for presentation, opportunities to write articles for publication, and invitations to volunteer for committee assignments. We are all conscious of our professional reputations and if we are even moderately interested in improving them, we will be prepared to make an effort to enhance them by whatever means seem appropriate. Reviewing is simply one effective way to get your name before the profession while at the same time polishing and perfecting your writing skills.

Assuming you make a success of reviewing and end up with obligations to provide reviews for several publications, what do you do with the books you receive after you've read them? It is generally understood that the review copy is yours to keep as a token of appreciation for having written the review. Keeping the works you review is a positive reward with some negative aspects. You can build an impressive collection of books and other materials in the areas in which your review, but that can lead to amassing a conglomeration of materials that will eventually be difficult to dispose of when the time comes, and come it will. How will you know when your collection has reached critical mass? When your roommate/husband/mistress/lover/live-in threatens to have you committed if you so much as accept another review copy? Depending upon what you review, there may be a few useful reference titles to save, but to keep your sanity and close associates, you'll want to keep the books moving on to other more appropriate repositories.

The IRS must be considered if you decide to donate certain reviewed materials to institutions. Be sure to keep accurate records of the value of the materials donated and, if you decide to claim them on your income tax, be sure to get an opinion from your tax advisor beforehand. Did you receive the books as payment for services rendered? Did you declare them as earned income? These and other questions are ones that your tax advisor can assist you in answering.

The personal rewards and opportunities that reviews can lead to are substantial. Reviewing can provide the recognition already alluded to. It can also help you develop expertise in writing and can actually enforce a new writing discipline. You will have to learn to observe accurately and report clearly and concisely. You'll have to be able to meet deadlines, sometimes, at least from your point of view, very short-term deadlines. You will have to learn to write in an acceptable, often cogent style, rigorously trimming excess verbiage from each and every sentence and paragraph. You will, of necessity, have to keep in touch with current publishing trends in the areas in which you review, and through this new awareness, you'll expand your expertise accordingly.

Your well-written reviews can also lead to requests for article submissions in the area of your reviewing specialty. As you become more proficient, you may be asked to write reviews on a paid basis. As you become better known and more capable as a reviewer, you may be approached by a publisher who is looking for individuals knowledgeable in specific subject areas who are willing to serve as paid readers, reviewing manuscripts currently under consideration for publication. There's usually a small fee attached to such offers as well as more recognition.

ABANDONING REVIEWING

Eventually, you may arrive at a point where you must consider abandoning reviewing. Why would you do such a thing after all the time and effort taken to break into the reviewing field? We're sure you'll have good reasons.

When Enough Is Enough

One reason to abandon review writing is that you may simply burn out. If you reach the point where the sight of just one more package from the your review editor makes you sick, you have reached the burn-out stage. If you find reading for pleasure is no longer a pleasure when the bottom line is another review, maybe you have been reviewing too much and you need a rest. If you simply have no time to review because of your commitments elsewhere, that's yet another reason to cease reviewing. If your review style is no longer appropriate to the periodical, perhaps because of a management change, or a change brought about by the evolution of your own writing style, it's time to switch to something else. How you go about dropping out is very important, especially if you want to leave the door ajar so you can return later on.

Bowing Out Gracefully

If you decide to abandon your reviewing, don't just drop your commitments abruptly. Whether you cease activity because of your own personal reasons, a change in your commitments, or because you had a tiff with an editor, bow out gracefully. As soon as you decide to stop reviewing, write a polite letter to the editor informing him/her of your decision. Keep all your contacts and correspondence on a friendly, cheerful level whether or not you actually feel that way. Offer to stay on a little longer if the editor needs time to locate a replacement. Keep in mind that you wanted an opportunity to review books not too long ago, and you were given the chance. Now that you want to leave, you've got something of an obligation to do it as gracefully as possible. That means giving your editor plenty of advance notice to make new arrangements. You want to keep your record of responsibility and dependability intact. If you intend to return to reviewing for this particular publication several years from now, there may be a new crew of editors, but your former reviewing record will be on file and will go a long way toward getting you reinstated.

It is not a bad idea to keep the review process going by continuing to produce reviews for at least one review source, even on an infrequent basis. However, if your intent to quit entirely is irreversible, make sure you keep a file of some examples of your published reviews so you can use them if and when you decide to reenter the review market.

SOME HINTS ABOUT WRITING REVIEWS

Make up your mind early on not to review books where there might be any suggestion of a possible conflict of interest. Conflicts of interest come in a variety of shapes and sizes and some are not always easily identifiable. You have to be careful and have the conflict-of-interest concern issue uppermost in your mind every time you contemplate a new book to review. Examples of conflict of interest include a personal connection with the author or publisher or a strong prejudice against the author or the viewpoint expressed—a prejudice so strong that you know you are not going to be objective. If you think you've got a possible conflict of interest with a particular book, give your editor a call and explain your concern. Follow the editor's advice even if it means returning the book and shredding the review that you've just completed.

Be prepared to read all of a monograph, whether fiction or nonfiction. Skimming the work and borrowing extensively from the publisher's release or book jacket may get the job done, but it will not result in your best work and, as such, is a practice to avoid. Be prepared to expend the time examining reference works or bibliographies adequately enough to critique the work fairly. This process will include comparing the work with others that are similar in topic or coverage. When you finish your review and after making this thorough analysis, you'll feel like an expert on this particular work and indeed you will be. You'll be confident of your knowledge, and you'll end up writing a good review as a result.

Pay special attention to the table of contents, the introduction, the preface, or other preliminary material that may state the author's purpose in writing or compiling the work. It is unfair to criticize an author for not meeting the objectives for the book if they were clearly stated in the introduction and you missed them altogether. If you are going to criticize an error of omission or commission, take care to get your facts absolutely straight before you make your point in print.

Avoid writing clichés! Keep your style fresh and original. Don't concentrate your attention on the number of pages per chapter, personal concerns about arrangement (although arrangement is important to the coherence of the work), or irrelevant ramblings about layout (although severe problems with the quality of the production should always be noted). Ignore minor flaws that are irrelevant to the work as a whole. If there are major or significant problems with the work, state them, but don't dwell on insignificant details that don't detract from the overall worth of the work.

Be prepared to check and recheck your facts. Readers will purchase or reject, use or ignore the work based on what you say in print. Be careful and be fair. Master the mechanics of reviewing. Read the press releases accompanying the materials looking for valuable clues about the intended audience. The background of the author may be noted in the press release and nowhere else. Read the preliminary matter in the book or the editorial pages of the new periodical you are reviewing. Examine the book jacket for similar information. As you read the book, make notes and bracket possible quotes, recording their pagination in your notes. Think of original approaches to use in writing the review as you evaluate the work. Be on the lookout for ways you can make your review enjoyable to the reader as well as informative.

Most review sources have very strict requirements regarding review length. That limitation may involve getting your clear, concise, and pithy review condensed to a mere 25 lines of double-spaced typescript in lines of no more than 38 characters in length. Many review sources supply copy paper that has the boundaries clearly drawn. Fitting your review into the tight, unyielding confines of the copy paper can be a frustrating exercise for the beginner. If you want to avoid problems the first time around, take some blank sheets of typing paper and, with a ruler, draw in the copy paper boundaries. Type your review on the practice sheets you've created and rework, cut, and revise until you are satisfied with the results. (You can also photocopy the supplied copy paper and use the copies as your practice sheets.) With the review completed on the practice paper, it is safe to retype your completed review on the copy paper, address it to your editor, and put it into the mail.

If you have access to a microcomputer or dedicated word processor, you can substitute the screen of the monitor for your practice paper and set up your copy paper format on the screen and then type, revise, move, and revise again until you've got exactly what you want. With the word processor, there is no need to wonder "Will it fit?" You'll know for certain before you ever commit it to paper. When it comes time to print it, depending on the hardware you have available, you could print it directly on the copy paper provided by the reviewing source or simply print it on regular 8½-by-11-inch paper, making as many copies as you need to satisfy your editor. Most editors have no problems accepting computer-printed reviews, but you should always ask first before submitting one.

The computer-generated review eliminates all of the manual labor and frustration involved in typing and retyping your reviews. Using the word processor to format, compose, and edit your review will cut your total preparation time by at least half. It may even help to improve the quality of your writing simply because it makes the revision process almost effortless.

One purpose of a review is to help potential readers or users of the work evaluate the relevance of the material for their specific needs. With this in mind, there are different types of reviews to consider. The summary review relates the contents of the work or indicates the scope. This type of review is factual in nature and does not necessarily divulge your opinion of the work. An evaluative review assesses the author's success in covering the topic; compares the work with others similar in nature; and indicates strengths, weaknesses, and readability. The evaluative review usually leads directly to a favorable or unfavorable recommendation. Keep those points in mind as you construct your comments.

Another purpose of reviewing books, periodicals, and other information tools is to build interest and promote sales. Obviously, a series of rave reviews will help place a given title on the best-seller list. Those positive reviews, many of which appear long before the book is released to the general public, help to create product demand. The book is a publisher's product and demand means sales which, in turn, lead to profits. By receiving positive reviews months before a book reaches the readers, bookstores and libraries place advance orders based in large part on how they interpreted the reviews—your reviews.

The negative review also sells books since libraries must cover all viewpoints on issues and must satisfy a variety of readers' tastes. That means that even though your review paints the book in a negative light, your analysis, as critical as it is, will not necessarily restrict sales. It may actually attract buyers. If you must write a negative review (and you will find you often must), be fair in the manner in which you describe the negative aspects. At all times remember your role as a responsible, fair, and honest reviewer. You can't afford to indulge in casual, irresponsible, offhand comments.

If, until now, you thought the book review was a rather unimportant and insignificant appendage to the series of events that take a book from the forest to the library shelf, we hope you've got a new perspective and can see yourself as a potential part of that process. As a reviewer, you can add your talent to a respectable and needed art form and, at the same time, begin the process of getting your views and ideas into print. At the same time, you'll be polishing and refining your writing skills.

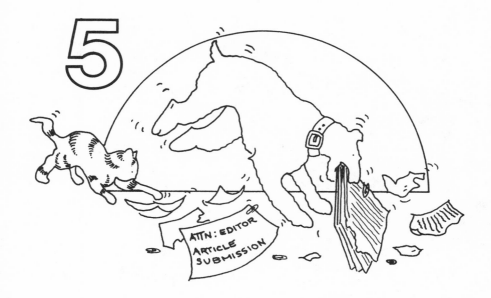

Writing and Publishing Articles

There are basically two ways to start the process of writing periodical articles. You can write the article first and then decide where to submit it, or you can decide in advance which periodicals you intend to target for your submissions. For example, let's assume you've had some success writing brief articles for a newsletter and now want to tackle a more ambitious project. You have decided that a periodical article of roughly 3,000 words is just about the right length, and you even have a topic in mind, something that occurred to you when you were writing for the newsletter but which was too long and detailed for your editor to consider.

CHOOSING YOUR TOPIC

Naturally, you want your article to be a success, and one of the best ways to ensure success is to stick to topics about which you are familiar and with which you are comfortable. It's easiest (and more enjoyable for you) to write from personal experience. But don't let unfamiliarity with a topic dissuade you from writing about it. Instead, do the research and reading necessary to write a solid, informative article. The more you know about the topic in advance of any writing, the better your chances are of getting your editor's and, ultimately, your readers' attention.

Once you have settled on a topic, you will want to attempt to predict the kind of competition you can expect to face from other authors. Is it already a popular topic? Is it one that other authors are currently writing about? If it is, does what you have to say add significantly to the current body of knowledge? If it does, you clearly have a reason to write your article. If it doesn't, you might as well drop the topic and look for another one. Determining the level of interest in your topic takes some effort but is well worth your time.

AUTHOR GUIDELINES

Assuming you've tentatively identified a few likely prospects for your work, what happens next? You start looking for the exact publication requirements of each periodical title you've identified to obtain additional information concerning the nature of articles accepted; style and grammar rules; and specifications on photographs, article length, and subject focus.

Some of the periodicals you might be considering, such as *Library Acquisitions: Practice and Theory,* print their author guidelines in each issue. Others print their guidelines separately and make them available upon request. A representative selection of author guidelines is provided in an appendix to this book.

With the proper guidelines available, you will be able to do a more thorough job of evaluating your tentative periodical selections. After comparing each set of author guidelines to the concept of your article, you'll almost certainly be able to narrow your list of periodicals even more.

This is also the time to gather a few back issues of the periodical(s) in question and review them to see if you can imagine your article fitting in with the ones in print. In most cases, you'll have no trouble deciding how or if your article will fit in. Looking over the back issues and reading the author guidelines will provide you with sufficient background to help you decide whether or not to go on to the next step.

THE QUERY LETTER

Now, before you actually begin writing, is a good time to send the all-important query letter to the editor of the periodical(s) you have selected in order to determine whether or not your proposed article would be of interest. (The author guidelines may even suggest that you write the query letter.) Some editors would much rather know what you have in mind before receiving an unsolicited manuscript in the mail. In response to your query letter, the editor may tell you that, although the article you are contemplating has merit and is of interest to librarians, it just so happens that, within the last six months, dozens of other authors have chosen to write on the same topic. All of a sudden, the market potential for your proposed article has fallen to zero. Although the pessimist would become discouraged at this point, the optimist (you) is relieved to learn what to many would be seemingly disappointing news. Had the article been written without consulting the editor, valuable time would have been wasted for all parties involved.

CHOOSING A TITLE AND OTHER CAVEATS

We are assuming that your writing skills are sufficiently well honed to allow you to produce a readable article. We also assume that you are willing to follow the rules for preparing your manuscript as set forth in the author guidelines for the periodical(s) to which you intend to send your article. With those important points understood, we can turn to several other considerations, one of which is choosing a title for your article. Choosing a title is about as important as getting an acceptance from the editor of your choice. An obvious exaggeration, you say. Not really, when you consider how important the title can be as an attraction to potential readers. You want your article to be read and, beyond that, you want your article to be cited in other publications. Not only is having your article cited frequently good for your ego, it is also good for the librarian-author who is interested in building a network, making contacts, and, in general, becoming a recognized name in the profession. The more articles you write and the more frequently they are cited, the more widely you will be recognized. We will deal with citations and the importance of recognition in Chapter 10, "Establishing Your Reputation."

And what does that article title have to do with citations and getting people to read your article? Readers of professional literature, in particular, regularly skim periodicals looking for interesting articles. If they don't look at the actual articles, they will at least read the table of contents. If you seriously want others to search out and read your article, then you are going to have to attract their attention with a thought-provoking title that will be too interesting to pass by. Titles that lack the magic words that spark interest, no matter how well written or interesting the article, are not likely to be given a second glance.

What can the author do to make a title attractive? Include carefully selected keywords that identify exactly what you are writing about. It will take some time to get precisely the title you want, but it will be time well spent. Make a list of half a dozen titles and juggle the keywords around until there can be no mistake about the message you want to get across. You might even ask a colleague to read your list of titles and pick the most interesting in the event you have trouble selecting. When the casual reader skims the table of contents in which your article is listed, the title you've selected will be a paragon of clarity, and its subject will be recognized at once. The reader may decide to pass it up but not because the title failed to communicate the subject.

While we're on the topic of titles, there is another good reason to design your article title carefully. When your article is indexed, the indexers assign subject headings or keyword descriptors to your article, and it is those descriptors that link your article with the subject headings in the published index. A clear, easily indexed title will make the professional indexer's job far easier and will help to ensure that your article will be listed under those subject headings where interested readers and researchers will find it quickly and easily.

WRITING REPORTS

A report is another kind of article that offers a variety of prospects for publication. Writing a report of a meeting, conference, or some other event takes considerable practice and patience but will provide another excellent opportunity for practice and skill-building.

Reports are read primarily for their informational value; therefore, the writer/reporter must be a careful observer and a willing recorder of accurate detail. Taking minutes in a committee meeting is an excellent way to break into report writing. If you want to write reports, but you are unsure of your ability to handle the amount of detail, bring along a portable tape recorder for the first one or two sessions. Take your notes, but run the tape recorder as a backup. After you have written your report from your notes, review the tape and see what, if anything, you have missed. After doing this a few times, you will begin to sort out the important aspects of each meeting and capture them in your notes without having to rely on the tape recorder. Don't overdo it, however. Once your colleagues find out that you've become a superior minute-taker, you'll be overwhelmed with requests to serve as secretary for every committee in sight!

Special attention to your own personal writing style is important if your report is going to be read and understood. If the subject is of vital importance, people will manage to read your report no matter how badly it's written. But if the meeting or event is of a routine nature, it's going to be up to you, the reporter, to make the report interesting and readable and still factual. This you will accomplish by perfecting a straightforward, journalistic style which makes the transfer of information from you to your readers a simple and easily understood process. Clear, concise, and accurate reporting attracts more readers and, ultimately, results in a high level of reader satisfaction and understanding. These should be your objectives if this is the kind of article you intend to write.

As your reporting assignments increase both in number and complexity, you'll still want to keep the tape recorder handy in order to pick up critical portions of events from which you might like to quote extensively. If you are going to insert a quotation, verbatim, you *must* be accurate. The tape recorder is a great insurance policy when it comes to including every word of the quotation cited.

ADDING THE VISUAL TO THE WRITTEN WORD

You'll also want to consider carrying a camera in order to provide photographs with which to supplement or enhance your articles. Reporting at conferences offers excellent opportunities for taking photographs that you can use to supplement your articles or even sell to other publications. Taking quality photographs is not a creative activity limited to the professional photographer. Lots of so-called amateurs do it regularly with surprisingly impressive results. If you've avoided photography to supplement your writing simply because you are not a photographer, just remember that you are not a professional journalist either, but you can learn.

Using a 35mm camera is not quite as simple as point and shoot, but the technology has almost advanced to that stage. There are any number of perfectly reliable cameras selling for under $200 which are exceptionally easy to operate yet provide publication quality results.

With the technology in hand, the reporter/photographer needs only to work out a system or routine that will result in consistently reliable photography on every reporting assignment. Here are some suggestions to follow in setting up your own system:

- Choose a simple-to-operate 35mm camera with a built-in flash and exposure metering system. If you want to simplify things even further, choose a model with automatic focus. This is the ultimate point-and-shoot model, and it works especially well when you are in a hurry and don't have time to focus. Become thoroughly familiar with the operation of the camera and shoot several rolls of film before you ever take it on a reporting assignment.
- Locate a photo lab that is convenient to your base of operation and work out an arrangement with the proprietor to develop your film and provide you with publication quality enlargements. You will have to pay more for this kind of service, but you won't regret the investment. The kind of

mass production film processing associated with your local drugstore film service won't provide the quality you need.

- Choose one brand and speed of 35mm black-and-white film and stick with it. Your quality photo processor will use consistent, reliable developing lab procedures that will ensure continuous quality. By keeping your film processing and film speed and brand constant, you'll soon be able to tell exactly what kind of quality photographs you can expect under a variety of conditions. Kodak Tri-X black-and-white film with its ASA film speed of 400 is a great, all-purpose film to use with your reporting assignments.

- Avoid color film. It may look great in family album prints or in slides projected on the dining room wall, but for your specific publication purposes, black-and-white film provides just the right kind of graphic contrast and quality that reproduces well in print.

- At large conferences, visit the press booth and let the staff know that you are interested in taking photographs and for what purpose. They may ask you to register and may even give you a press badge which will legitimize your camera. At smaller meetings, be sure to ask the sponsor or speaker(s) for permission to photograph and be ready to abide by their response. You'll usually get a chance to take your pictures, but if you are refused permission, don't be persistent.

- Whenever possible, try to get your photos without using your flash attachment. Flashing strobes can drive some sensitive speakers right off the platform. Try to get your speaker photos early in the presentation and then put the camera away.

Reporting can become a pretty complex activity at large conferences, so don't take on more than you can handle, particularly if you'll also be taking pictures. The people at the press booth usually have a good supply of press releases that appear throughout the conference, and they are usually willing to mail you copies of releases that appear after the conference has concluded. You might even want to get on their mailing list so you can refer to releases describing events that you were unable to attend.

WRITING THE HOW-TO OR APPLICATIONS ARTICLE

If there was ever a popular format for members of the information science field, this is it. This, in its worst form, is the old how-we-do-it-at-Siwash-U article which frequently borders on reinventing the wheel. Because there is little in the way of standardization in the library profession when it comes to developing procedures for problem solving, there are endless opportunities for articles describing innovative and creative methods for handling common problems. These are relatively easy to write and usually follow the "problem statement and solution offered" format. They frequently lend themselves to the incorporation of photographs, diagrams, and flowcharts. The best of them offer unique solutions to real problems and can be useful to the practical librarian looking for solutions instead of theories and philosophy. If you have a valuable how-to experience to share, here are some suggestions to follow as you develop it into an article:

- Make certain that someone following your instructions can replicate the situation you describe. Have a friend who knows something about the process you are outlining read it to spot errors or omissions.
- Don't write about something that doesn't have an application in many other institutions. So you did something unique at your library? If it has no application anywhere else, who cares?
- Make certain that drawings, photographs, charts, and related artwork are clear, sharp, and really do serve to illustrate your point. They should enhance or supplement obviously and clearly, otherwise, don't include them.
- Check out your "innovation" before you write it up. You may not have discovered anything new at all. Others may have been there first, in fact, a number of times!
- If you are describing something that others have done, give them appropriate credit, even if it comes to sharing the authorship. Just because someone else did whatever it is you are describing doesn't mean you should forget writing about it. Go ahead, by all means, but give all the principals their due.

The how-to is fun to write, and if it provides useful information, there's a steady demand for it.

THE SCHOLARLY ARTICLE

If you are an academic librarian under a "publish or perish" edict, your writing will probably lean toward a scholarly approach. Having selected the scholarly publication of your choice as a target for your article, be extremely careful as you begin writing in order to avoid one fairly common pitfall—becoming so involved with the details of scholarly writing that you lose sight of your thesis and, ultimately, your audience. Yours is going to be a formal paper citing the works of others and addressing your topic according to a particular style. Watch out for the tendency to forget your message or lose sight of your objective and take considerable pains to make sense, both grammatically and logically, as you follow the traditional form and format. If you are unsure of your premise or in doubt about the validity of your conclusion, ask a friend to critique your article for you. Friends do have a tendency to want to please, however, so instead, you might prefer to ask a willing colleague whose opinion you respect. S/he is more likely to render an honest judgment since a friendship is not at stake.

ORGANIZATION AND STRUCTURE

While the scholarly article follows a relatively predictable, pre-scribed pattern, the informational, journalistic report and how-to articles don't have such formal restrictions. If you want your articles to be accepted by editors and read and understood by your intended audience, you'll have to follow a few basic rules.

Start off with a description of the problem, project, or situation. Describe what took place and then wrap it up with a conclusion. Having a well-defined beginning, middle, and conclusion is part of the process of taking the reader into the article, based on what you intend to describe in the main body of the article, describing it, and then taking the reader out. Conclusions should offer suggestions for further reading, caveats, and other devices to bring the article to an obvious ending. You'll have your own methods for writing each article, but as long as you answer the questions you pose and take the reader logically through a series of events in clear, straightforward English sentences, you'll have the makings of a highly readable article.

SUBMITTING YOUR ARTICLE

If you've got more than one prospective periodical editor willing to review your submission, how do you decide which one gets first refusal? You have a personal interest in getting your article read by as many of your colleagues as possible. As you consider this point, start narrowing the field by applying a few standards of your own. Is the periodical indexed? If so, where? Does it have wide circulation? Is it cited frequently? Is it where you turn to locate current, topical articles? By asking yourself a few questions, you can easily come up with a priority order for your submission. Yes, you could send a copy to all three, but that won't make many friends, especially when your article is accepted by all three and you're faced with the prospect of turning two of them down. (For more about multiple submissions, see Chapter 7, "Writing and Publishing a Book.") When submitting articles, do so one at a time. If you think an editor has taken too long to reply to your submission, write or call for a status report. Editors like to have a supply of articles on hand and ready for publication; it gives them flexibility and a sense of security as they design future issues. Your article may be ready to go to press in May, but the editor might decide to hold it until December because it can be used with a special thematic issue. There are also editors who accept articles submitted in good faith and then never publish them. Such editors are evasive and prefer to keep the author guessing. Once you discover such an editor, plan to avoid him/her in the future.

The physical format of your submission is something to keep in mind as you look over the final product. Have you followed the author guidelines carefully? Have you prepared the two copies required? Is your complete name, address, and telephone number included with your submission? Is the final product easy to read? Many articles are typed or printed using ribbons that should have been tossed into the nearest wastebasket months ago. The result is a faint image that requires incredible concentration to read. Even though the author guidelines allow submission of manuscripts printed on dot matrix printers, those older printers that deliver character sets that do not have descenders (the tail on the letter "q," for example, does not print below the line) will produce a very unattractive and hard-to-read manuscript. If you think the editor will have to struggle in order to read your work, find another way to produce it. Don't send it in until it is as near perfection as you can make it.

If your article is going to be rejected, let it be for content or philosophical reasons and not for some simple mechanical problem that you could have easily recognized and eliminated. In most cases, your submission is competing with those of many other authors. The more ways you can find to eliminate those little mechanical problems, the more time you'll have to concentrate on the important part of your writing effort: the content.

THE INTERVIEW

Interviewing is a form of reporting, with a question-and-answer approach that puts you, the interviewer, into the picture in a one-to-one (or in some instances one-to-more-than-one) relationship requiring you to be more than just a writer.

The interview can be something as detailed and scholarly as an oral history project in which every utterance is important and where editing is minimal because every word counts. In other instances, getting the essence of the interviewee's comments becomes the important aspect of the interview, and consequently, the interviewer will have considerable freedom to edit the final transcript. Yet another variation of the interview places the interviewer in a truly creative writing situation in which the observations and opinions of the interviewer become a basic ingredient of the interview. A good example of this type of interview can be found in *Publishers Weekly,* "PW Interviews," in which the bulk of the interview consists of the reporter's observations liberally sprinkled with quotations from the person interviewed.

Whatever format you select, you'll find that it will require you to use both your editing and writing talents. Reading interviews of interesting or well-known personalities has an appeal that never seems to end.

Aside from having an interesting subject and a thoroughly relaxed, nerveless interviewer, what makes a successful interview? Trust is probably the most important element in any successful interview. If the interviewer and interviewee don't have it, the interview itself can become an uncomfortable and unrewarding experience. Almost every interviewee is worried about saying something unflattering or damaging that will end up in print. It is up to the interviewer to determine how far to go in the process of deleting potentially awkward or unflattering comments. If they are left in, they present a more realistic picture of the interviewee. If they are edited out, the interviewee will be forever in your debt; however, your finished product may lack a good deal of realism.

In editing a newsletter (*Technicalities*), our personal policy has always been to make certain that the interviewee understands that fumbles and blunders can and will be corrected before publication. We find that, for *Technicalities*, a truly successful interview requires that both the interviewer and the interviewee be satisfied with the results. That means that if a question or answer needs to be deleted before publication in order to satisfy the interviewee, then it should be done. A number of editors and interviewers will take issue with this approach, but we are conducting our interviews in the information science profession and not engaging in the kind of investigative reporting that might characterize an interview, for example, on a CBS "60 Minutes" broadcast.

What do you need to consider when preparing to undertake an interview?

- First and foremost, read John Brady's 1976 book, *The Craft of Interviewing* (listed in the bibliography at the end of this book).
- Give your interviewee a set of questions well in advance of the interview so that s/he can spend a little time thinking about the topics you want to discuss.
- Arrange to have your interview conducted in a quiet area free from interruptions. Avoid restaurants and other public places where background noises can compete with your subject.
- Use an unintimidating, compact, reliable tape recorder that can handle standard, 90-minute cassettes. Make sure it will operate on either batteries or with a transformer from a

standard 110-volt outlet. Test it under every imaginable interview situation before you sit down to tape the real thing.

- Don't rely on the built-in ceramic microphones found on many portable tape recorders. They don't produce a quality recording that can be transcribed easily. Instead, purchase a quality microphone that is designed to pick up normal room conversation. There's a new flat, credit-card-size, battery-operated microphone from Radio Shack that is especially sensitive and well-suited to interviewing. Because it is small and flat, it is not intimidating (large, studio-type microphones often are) and makes an excellent choice both from the standpoint of portability and its inconspicuous presence.
- Plan to stop the tape and give your interviewee a breather every so often. That's a good time to check the tape to make sure you are getting a satisfactory recording.

Try to transcribe the tape directly onto floppy disks so you'll be able to edit it on your word processor with relative ease. If you don't have the equipment, a typed transcription will have to suffice, but be prepared to create several drafts as you edit. When you are satisfied with the results, and depending on the type of interview you have conducted and the understanding you have with your interviewee, you may want to send him/her a copy for correction and approval. There's always the worry that the interviewee will cut material that you would like to keep or will want to completely rewrite the interview, but that's a chance you'll have to take if your objective is to produce an interview that will ultimately satisfy both parties.

Chances are you can't tape an interview again if something goes awry, so you'll need to take every conceivable precaution to ensure a successful interview. Be sure to:

- Confirm all of your interview appointments.
- Make sure you have identified a quiet spot for an uninterrupted interview session.
- Carry extra tape cassettes and a spare set of batteries.
- Check all of your equipment in advance to make sure it is all there and in top operating condition.
- Label your completed tapes the minute you are finished and keep them in a safe place until it's time to have them transcribed.
- If your interview involves air travel, consider taking precautions around airport security equipment by keeping your finished tapes in a lead-lined bag of the type used for photographic film and hand carry the bag for inspection by security personnel.

Interviews can be very entertaining and informative for the reader, but they require a tremendous amount of typing and editing before they are ready for the printer. To make sure that all goes well from the beginning, the interviewer will have to play several roles ranging from diplomat, interrogator, confidant, and improvisor to director, technician, writer, and editor. It is demanding work but well worth the investment in planning and editing.

Compiling and Publishing Bibliographies

Compilation of bibliographies is a pursuit enjoyed by many and abhorred by others. Some people enjoy the identification of resources, the tracking down of elusive citations, the writing of annotations—others are miserable even contemplating doing it.

For those who enjoy bibliography compilation, there are real rewards in pulling together hundreds of publications on a specific topic and arranging them in a format useful to researchers. There is a feeling of accomplishment in observing the final product being used and knowing that you have become an expert on a particular subject or a narrow facet of a subject.

A person interested in bibliography work must be persistent by
nature, determined to see the project through to its conclusion, creative in identifying citations, succinct and analytical in writing the
annotations, and willing to devote months or years to the research.

There are different types of bibliographies. Descriptive/analytic
bibliographies cover every conceivable aspect of a text or body of
work, including physical descriptions of the work. An example of this
type of bibliography might be a work detailing an important private
collection of rare books. The other type of bibliography, and the kind
we will be focusing on in this chapter, is the systematic bibliography.
Systematic bibliographies can be of two types: enumerative or subject.
An enumerative bibliography is an inventory, such as the work of an
author, or it may be a national or trade bibliography such as *British
Museum*. A subject bibliography covers a particular subject, such as
literary criticism of the 1920s. Periodical indexes and abstracting
services can also be considered subject bibliographies.

IDENTIFYING CITATIONS

Compilation of a bibliography can be extremely time-consuming
and tedious. However, there are several advantages to entering the
world of publishing by first compiling a bibliography. The time
necessary to produce a bibliography on a subject is likely to be much
less than that needed to write a monograph or other narrative. The
actual publication production time is also likely to be less than for a
monograph. Bibliographies have a built-in market so a certain sales
level can be anticipated: The academic libraries will buy the bibliography, many on an automatic basis, in order to satisfy the needs of
the academic community. Finally, production of a bibliography is
inexpensive from a publisher's viewpoint since many bibliographies
are produced from camera-ready copy.

If you decide that compilation of a bibliography is the publication route you wish to take, first consider the field of bibliography
itself. How does one compile a bibliography? There are two excellent
background sources with which the novice bibliographer should become familiar.

First is a publication entitled "Guidelines for the Preparation of
a Bibliography" which was approved by the Reference and Adult
Services Division of the American Library Association in July 1982.
The guidelines are based on "Criteria for Evaluating a Bibliography"
which was endorsed by the Reference Services Division Board in
1971. These guidelines are intended for evaluators of bibliographies
as well as the actual compilers of bibliographies and their publishers.
They are intended for online and printed bibliographies and are also
used by other groups. Another background source that is practical in
approach is an article by A. J. Colaianne entitled "The Aims and

Methods of Annotated Bibliography," published in *Scholarly Publishing*. The elements of compilation are detailed in the article as well as an evaluation of the purposes of a bibliography. Other sources of information on bibliography compilation are listed in the bibliography at the end of this book.

SELECTING THE TOPIC

It may sound obvious, but the first item of business for the potential bibliographer is to identify the subject of the bibliography. Yes, it sounds obvious, but it isn't necessarily that easy to do. The subject must meet several criteria.

- The subject must be one that the compiler is knowledgeable of and in which s/he has some expertise. This expertise may be derived from an actual degree in the field (preferably an advanced degree), extensive research in the field, an intense interest in the subject, and a knowledge of research already performed.
- The subject should be one about which no bibliography has been previously compiled; should be a topic which has been the focus of significant, recent research; or should be a subject where you can clearly document the inadequacy of existing sources.
- The subject should be one in which there is some interest currently or a subject that has a clearly defined market. If you are interested in compiling a bibliography on playa lakes, for example, be sure that there is enough of an interest in the subject.
- It should be one in which there is a need for a bibliography. For example, as enrollments drop and financing patterns for higher education are being examined, there might be a need for a bibliography on financing of higher education.
- The subject should be one for which there is material readily available, especially in the general area where you, the compiler, work. You may have to make trips to other libraries to obtain access to material but, the more available to you locally, the easier compilation will be for you. This is critical when it comes to meeting a publisher's deadlines.

A subject that is popular, topical, and current is always of potential interest to publishers. A bibliography that complements popular works or could be considered "trendy" will have instant appeal. This appeal will, of course, be contingent upon your being able to produce a bibliography *in time* to meet rising interest. You may form the habit of keeping a folder titled "ideas" or "future bibliographies" where you place reminder notes about potential subjects. These ideas will come to you as you work at the reference desk answering questions or as you have private brainstorming sessions.

As you consider your subject, also consider the time commitment you must be prepared to make. Can you invest the time needed to produce a book-length project? If the bibliography is for a handout or for a periodical, is there too much time involved in preparing a respectable bibliography for it to be worthwhile for you to do?

STATEMENT OF INTENT

Once you have selected your subject, how do you begin? Begin by constructing a systematic statement of what will be included/excluded in your bibliography and why. From this, you can develop a scheme for arranging your bibliography. If it is a topic in which you are interested, you probably have the beginnings of a bibliography already in the form of citations you've noted over the years. You may also get a good beginning list of citations and abstracts by doing an online search—using BRS, WILSONLINE, or DIALOG—of your topic and related subjects. Then as you begin seeking those citations, you will find other relevant articles, books, etc., to include.

As you begin compiling the bibliography, have in mind how comprehensive it will be, whether it will cover a specific time period, the reasons for inclusion and exclusion of certain items, and what other constraints you are exercising in choosing material for inclusion. What will be the primary focus of the bibliography? This is important because as you complete the compilation, you will have to write an introduction to the work in which you state your methodology, present an overview of the topic, describe the organization of the work and the role the indexes play in providing access, and the degree of selectivity you exercised in the compilation. You may also want to include an introduction written by another scholar in the field, an introduction that will explain the importance of your bibliographic work to the field of research on that topic.

It is important to define the time period you will be covering. Select a beginning date and, even more important, determine your ending date. Without an ending date or deadline, your compilation can continue indefinitely. There are numerous aspiring bibliographers collecting data who have not established a cutoff date for their collecting of citations. Until they do, they will continue to gather data that may never reach publication and may never provide assistance to other researchers. In addition, they could very well be "scooped" by other researchers who are willing to identify a specific time period, collect the data, and publish them.

TRACKING DOWN CITATIONS

As you gather data, you may find it more helpful to keep articles and books separate, gathering like data in specific research sessions. Lengthy sessions collecting article citations from indexing and abstracting services, followed by time spent in periodical stacks, can be interspersed by intervals standing at the card catalog or online catalog, noting call numbers. Your own techniques for efficient use of your time will evolve as you compile your initial bibliography. You will experience the frustration of trying to locate mystery or elusive citations. In the course of developing your techniques, you must determine how extensive your searching for potential dead ends will be. Some titles may not be able to be found. And no matter how exhaustive you attempt to be, someone will always know of additional materials you might have included if you had known of their existence.

There may be a two- to three-year lag time before articles are cited. Certainly there will be a lag time of several weeks or months after publication before they appear in the indexing and abstracting services. Once you have obtained the citations of articles or books and have determined that they are not available in your library or in the immediate area, you should consult a bibliographic utility, such as OCLC if available, or other national bibliographies, to identify the location of a copy of the material. If you must obtain the material on interlibrary loan, you know in advance that you will be facing a delay. The more of these difficult-to-locate items you can identify early on and request access to, the better. Even so, some will remain elusive, and you may have to contact colleagues in other libraries for assistance, list the item with no annotation, or omit it altogether. Sometimes you may have to rely on a secondary source such as a published abstract or a book review for items that appear significant but to which you cannot obtain access.

Even with the use of online identifying tools, such as database searches, or of location tools, such as bibliographic utilities, extensive manual searching will still be necessary, particularly for older items. There is no substitute for this manual labor even though online databases and expanding technology have made some of the initial identification and location easier.

Previously, the only method of compilation readily available to the bibliographer was creation of a card file of citations with the annotations added as the literature was examined. Now with the availability of microcomputers, bibliographies can be compiled using word processing packages or one of the relatively new bibliography programs. An example of such a bibliography program which utilizes index terms is Personal Bibliographic System (Personal Bibliographic Software, Inc., P.O. Box 4250, Ann Arbor, MI 48106). Other packages are also available, as well as some database management software packages found in many computer stores. Investigating these alternatives to the manual card file is worthwhile. By using an online compilation method, you will find that you are not only listing your citations and providing the annotations but you are also creating the final manuscript without endless retyping, editing, and proofreading.

AIMING TOWARD COMPLETENESS

Whatever your method of compilation, aim toward completeness and accuracy in your citations. Don't abbreviate authors' first names if you have any way of identifying what the name actually is. Provide a full title of the article, chapter, or book without truncation. Be sure to give the full title of the periodical or book in which the article or chapter appears. Don't assume that everyone knows what a journal abbreviation is. If abbreviations are used, for whatever reason, be sure to draw them from standard *published* sources, such as Modern Language Association (MLA) or in the Wilson indexes, such as *Readers Guide* or *Education Index.*

Also, take care to be complete and accurate in identifying such important parts of the citation as the volume number, date of publication, and pagination. Don't make assumptions about the expertise of the user. Adopt a citation style and stick to it throughout the bibliography. For journals, always include the volume number; if pagination begins anew with each issue, be sure to give the issue number or date of publication. Don't abbreviate pagination with a beginning page number and the letter "f" or "ff" to indicate the article or chapter continues on subsequent pages. Make the citation as exact as possible. If you identify the citation from another work, confirm the existence of the publication you want to cite and check the accuracy of the citation in an index. It is easy to create "ghost" citations through inaccurate information. Indeed, there have been instances of "ghost" citations being created to flesh out research. Be sure the citations you include are not "ghosts."

When you write the annotations, make sure they do not express your personal opinions or prejudices. Simply relate the gist of the article, chapter, or book, summarizing it cogently and thoroughly. Don't use what Colaianne calls "bibliographic Indian talk."[1] If you cannot easily paraphrase the article or book, quote accurately from the source, indicating that it is a quotation.

Don't write your citation from too cursory a review of the material. However, you cannot read the text of every item included in a 2,000-item bibliography so you will have to rely on quickly identifying the important ideas and the coverage without reading every word. You may also have to use abstracts. If you do not have access to the work, include it only if you can base inclusion on the importance of the work or the reputation of the author, author's affiliation, or the publication in which the material appears. When you do annotate, remember that it will be halpful to users to include whether the article or book has additional bibliographies itself, or what relevant illustrations are included, or that the work is a limited edition and therefore will be difficult to obtain. If the work you are annotating is controversial or unusually important, indicate that in your annotation, but don't express your own opinion of whether the thesis is accurate or not. Some bibliographers disagree on this subject. If you do choose to interject your own opinion, be prepared to have reviewers mention your "prejudice." Your role as a bibliographer is to provide a concise statement of content, not to editorialize.

How long should annotations be? Some schools of thought hold that a couple of hundred words is necessary for a book and under a hundred will summarize the average article. Ignore those word count guidelines. Your annotation should be the length that is necessary to adequately summarize the work for your audience.

If you are compiling for an English-speaking market but have identified some foreign language materials, provide a translation for the title in the body of your citation. Your English annotation will help the user of the bibliography determine whether or not it is worthwhile to locate the item and have the text translated.

GETTING/KEEPING ORGANIZED

As you identify the citations and write your annotations, it will probably be easier to keep the entries in an alphabetical manual or online file, assigning index terms as you work. After completing the research, you can then reorganize the cards by classification or reformat the online entries by index term.

You will have to determine a simple, appropriate organization for the bibliography. Don't create an overly complex structure with many subunits. A good source for classification is the *Library of Congress Subject Headings.* Other classification schemes might be based on key indexing or abstracting sources in the field in which you are working or the scheme might be entirely descriptive and of your own design. The more standard the classification is, the easier it will be for your user to use the work. Be simple. Many bibliographers prefer to rely on thesauri for their classification schemes. ERIC and *Psychological Abstracts* and other thesauri provide more depth in the subject than *Library of Congress Subject Headings* does. In addition, many of these thesaurus sources are also online. Your author, title, and subject indexes will provide access at a more complex level. Citation numbers will prove useful in accessing the materials through the indexes.

PUBLICATION SOURCES

Once you have decided on your topic, you should determine the audience for the finished project. Is this bibliography for use as a class handout? Do you anticipate publication in a periodical? Is it to be book length?

Class Handouts

If your audience is a class for which you are preparing a handout, don't be slothful in the compilation of the bibliography. Yes, the audience is "captive" but they deserve your best effort. And beginning to learn the techniques of bibliography compilation through preparing handouts will be helpful to you. Be sure the citations are for materials available within the library's collection or on reserve for the particular class. Nothing is more frustrating to a student than discovering that the interesting- or relevant-sounding citation is for an item that the library doesn't own, has never owned, and cannot obtain due to lack of availability or time constraints. Your class audience will appreciate it if you include the call numbers—accurately indicated—and any peculiar location information, such as the fact that the item is on reserve or is only available in the Architecture Library.

A bibliography compiled for a class will be shorter than one compiled for commercial publication. The annotations may be shorter since your expectation is that the class will go read the works for their own edification. Even though the bibliography is compiled for limited use, be sure it is readable and is presented in an attractive format (no pale photocopies, please). Keep in mind that the work going into the compilation of this brief class handout could be providing information which you can expand into a publication intended for a wider audience.

Periodicals

Before compiling a bibliography for a particular periodical, be sure that the editors of that publication are interested in publishing it. A letter of inquiry, describing your topic and why it is of current interest, especially to the audience of that journal, should be sent before doing anything else. If the periodical staff is not interested, then you have saved yourself time in compiling the bibliography or you know that you must find another publication source. You should also, before compiling a bibliography, examine recent issues of targeted publications to confirm that bibliographies are still being published in them.

There are periodicals in subject fields that will publish relevant bibliographies. A survey of the literature will determine if there is one in your area of interest. Some library periodicals publish bibliographies, a few of which are listed here; many of these publish bibliographic essays, not annotated bibliographies.

American Libraries. American Library Association, 50 E. Huron St., Chicago, IL 60611 (topical bibliographies).

Bulletin of Bibliography. Meckler Publishing, P.O. Box 405, Saugatuck Station, Westport, CT 06880 (bibliographies in humanities and social sciences).

Library Journal. R. R. Bowker, 205 E. 42nd St., New York, NY 10017 (topical bibliographies).

Reference Services Review. Pierian Press, Box 1808, Ann Arbor, MI 48106 (bibliographies of periodicals, by subject, region, etc.).

Serials Review. Pierian Press, Box 1808, Ann Arbor, MI 48106 (bibliographies of periodicals, by subject, region, etc.).

Wilson Library Bulletin. H. W. Wilson Company, 950 University Ave., Bronx, NY 10452 (topical bibliographies).

Books

If your interest is in publishing a book-length bibliography, there are several publishers known for publishing bibliographies. Review the catalogs of the following publishers and determine if they have published in areas similar to the one in which you plan to compile a bibliography. Approach those publishers first. Then, identify those publishers who might be interested in venturing into new bibliography areas.

ABC-Clio
  Box 4397
  Santa Barbara, CA 93103

ALA Publishing Services
  50 E. Huron St.
  Chicago, IL 60611

R. R. Bowker
  205 E. 42nd St.
  New York, NY 10017

Gale Research Co.
  Book Tower Building
  Detroit, MI 48226

Garland Publishing Inc.
  136 Madison Ave.
  New York, NY 10016

Greenwood Press
  88 Post Rd.
  P.O. Box 5007
  Westport, CT 06881

G. K. Hall and Co.
  70 Lincoln St.
  Boston, MA 02111

Knowledge Industry
  701 Westchester Ave.
  White Plains, NY 10604

Libraries Unlimited
P.O. Box 263
Littleton, CO 80160

Oryx Press
2214 N. Central
Phoenix, AZ 85004

McFarland & Company Inc.
Box 6111
Jefferson, NC 28640

Scarecrow Press
52 Liberty St.
Box 656
Metuchen, NJ 08840

After identifying prospective publishers, prepare a prospectus detailing the theme of the bibliography you plan to compile, the competition, the marketplace, the length, the time frame, whether or not it will be sent as camera-ready copy, and provide some sample citations. Also, indicate why you have the expertise to compile the bibliography, including your subject background or other proof of your expertise in the subject area, a listing of similar bibliographies you have compiled on related topics, and even the names of individuals who can vouch for your expertise.

While you are awaiting acceptance of your proposal for a book or periodical publication, you can keep busy identifying selections for the bibliography and determining your method of compilation. However, if you receive a flat rejection and have tried every possible source, be prepared to drop the research. But, don't destroy the work you have done. File it away. Its day may come and you may find other uses for the material.

Still other sources for publication are bibliography series, such as the Council of Planning Librarians series, the Oryx Bibliography Series: The Sciences, and the Vance bibliography series. Some publishers may even pay a fee to the compiler. Contacting the editors/publishers with letters of inquiry concerning the topic about which you wish to compile a bibliography is usually the best practice. Following are guidelines for the three bibliography series mentioned.

GUIDELINES FOR *COUNCIL OF PLANNING LIBRARIANS*

COUNCIL OF PLANNING LIBRARIANS

MERRIAM CENTER — 1313 E. 60TH STREET

CHICAGO, ILLINOIS 60637

(312) 947-2007/8

CALL FOR MANUSCRIPTS

The Council of Planning Librarians publishes bibliographies that pertain to an aspect of planning. We welcome contributions about the fields of architecture, economics, education environmental science, health science,

history, law, library science, political science, psychology, and
sociology that deal with the concerns of practicing planners and academic
researchers in the field of planning.

The following is a list of <u>suggested</u> topics for bibliographies. We
are receptive, however, to the broad range of topics that are of concern
to the planning community.

Adaptive Use
Advocacy Planning
After the Tornado...
Alternative Energy Development
Citizen Participation
Community Development
Comparative International Planning
District Heating
Economic Development and Management
Educational Program Planning
Environmental Planning
Fiscal Impact Studies
Forestry Use and Conservation
Housing
Human Services Delivery Systems
Land Use Planning

Natural Resources Conservation
Neighborhood Revitalization
Planning Administration
Planning as a Profession
Planning for the Elderly
Planning for the Shrinking City
Planning in Space
Planning Theory and Education
Public Sector/Private Sector Programs
Public Works
Rural Planning
Solid Waste Treatment and Disposal
Tax Incentives
Transportation Planning
Urban Design
Women and Planning/Women's Studies
Zoning

Take this opportunity to share your research information with your
colleagues and to be published by an international organization. Send your
proposals. (Remember that bibliographies that are current, topically
arranged, and annotated will receive the highest priority when being considered for potential publication.) As compensation for your contribution
to the CPL Bibliographies series, you will receive a $100 honorarium
and five complimentary copies of the published work. Authors will also
have the opportunity to make suggestions regarding the distribution of
promotional releases and review copies of their work.

For more information about publishing with CPL, please call or write:

Council of Planning Librarians
1313 East 60th Street
Chicago, IL 60637-2897
(312) 947-2007

BIBLIOGRAPHY GUIDELINES FOR MATERIAL SUBMITTED TO CPL

As described below, the four parts of a CPL bibliography usually are:
the introduction, the table of contents or (topic index), the citations,
and the annotations. If the material is lacking in some aspect, a revision
is suggested along these lines.

INTRODUCTION. The author should describe the research that generated the
bibliography; and should briefly discuss the organization of the bibliography, the nature of the citations (for example, the period covered
and the sources), comment on the present state of research on the topic,
and perhaps speculate on the future. There should be some mention about
what the bibliography offers the researcher in terms of its practicality
and uniqueness.

TABLE OF CONTENTS. A good table of contents categorizes the topic into
convenient and practical subcategories, and it facilitates use of the
bibliography for the reader. A breakdown by books, articles, documents,
etc. is useful only in a short bibliography and is less useful overall.

Such breakdowns are discouraged, though CPL has been flexible on this point. Sometimes a topic index is often better because it allows for a much finer breakdown of materials. It also facilitates typing and arrangement of the citations.

CITATIONS. Citations should cover the topic as completely as possible without including extraneous material. Two basic guidelines are dates and types of material. Generally citations are broken down by date and a cutoff date is suggested. Any material before that date should only be included if it is basic reference material or a "classic" in the field. The author should decide the cutoff date, but it is usually suggested that the date be 1970 or later. An overabundance of newspaper and popular magazine articles is considered extraneous. These and dissertations that are not annotated, at least in part, are undesirable. Other guidelines used are those that are suggested by members of the American Planning Association who often act as referees for manuscripts submitted to CPL. As long as all necessary information is in the citation, CPL is flexible about style, although the general format followed by CPL is that found in the University of Chicago's <u>The Chicago Manual of Style</u>. If the manuscript needs to be retyped by CPL, it is converted to that style.

ANNOTATIONS. Annotations are encouraged, even if they are only selective. They do not have to be complete sentences; however, CPL will edit the annotations for consistency and clarity of content. Annotations are <u>not</u> a prerequisite for publication.

Editor, CPL Bibliographies

Reprinted with permission of the Council of Planning Librarians.

GUIDELINES FOR *ORYX BIBLIOGRAPHY SERIES: THE SCIENCES*

About the Series

The *Oryx Bibliography Series: The Sciences* is a series of bibliographies designed to provide the most recent references on the current issues in the sciences. Each issue provides 200–250 fully annotated references along with a "Research Review" stating the history and state of the art of the topic being covered. The bibliographies provide the student or researcher with an introduction to the "hot" topics in the sciences. Each bibliography also contains a number of other features:

Evaluative Selection: Only the most important references are to be included. The bibliography does not strive to be comprehensive. **Fully Annotated:** References are to be annotated. **Readily Available Materials:** References chosen for inclusion should be available at most libraries throughout the United States. Obscure sources that are difficult to obtain are to be avoided. **Highly Current:** The bibliography should include the most recent materials so it is as up to date as possible. **Key Articles Highlighted:** Highlight the most important articles so that the user interested in only a few materials can key in to those that are the most useful. **Research Review:** A research review describing the state of the art of the subject being covered should precede the bibliography. **Undergraduate Level:** Only materials that are at the undergraduate student level are to be included. Do not include either technical or very general articles. **English Language Only:** Include only English language materials.

GUIDELINES FOR *VANCE BIBLIOGRAPHIES*

According to Mary Vance, editor, references may follow any format, however, the information must be accurate and the format consistent. Each bibliography that is accepted is retyped; the retyping may be from cards, manuscript, or printouts. Legibility is important, of course. The title should be descriptive. Publication is usually within three months of acceptance. An honorarium is paid and authors are supplied with copies of the published bibliography. Interested bibliographers should write to Vance Bibliographies; unsolicited bibliographies are also accepted on occasion.[2]

SELECTION OF A PUBLISHER

Selecting a publisher is no small consideration. If you plan to submit camera-ready copy (the preferred form for bibliographies), be sure you have the ability to provide such copy either through your own typing or inputting or by hiring someone to do it for you.

Be sure you know the amount in royalties you can expect, and don't expect to make a fortune from compilation of a bibliography. Ten percent royalty is fairly standard, although that figure is always subject to change. You should also ask your publisher how the bibliography will be marketed and be prepared as compiler to suggest where review copies should be sent and what mailing lists might be used for distribution of promotional flyers about the book.

TIME

Preparation of a bibliography is not only time-consuming but must be completed in a timely manner. You must beat any competition to the marketplace, and with a current topic, this may not be possible. Don't expect to take a leisurely few years completing a bibliography, unless you are compiling a comprehensive reference work that has no current relevancy.

Most compilations will need to be completed as quickly as possible, which is another reason to consider the use of a microcomputer. Once your idea has been accepted, be sure you can carve out time to complete the project expeditiously. You may have to use student assistants to do the preliminary legwork or use online databases to identify the initial citations. You may also need to visit other libraries to examine materials unavailable in your library or on interlibrary loan.

How much time should you allow? If you are employed full-time but can use some of your work hours to do research and write annotations, expect to spend about 20 percent of your week on the project. If you are an academic librarian, you may have some additional time available in the summer; nights and week-ends will also have to be used. Following such a schedule, expect to spend 18 months compiling a 2,000-plus citation, fully annotated, select bibliography. If you cannot use work time, lengthen the time frame.

If you are working with a collaborator(s), keep in mind that this collaboration may take extra time as citations are exchanged. One person must assume the coordinating role to make sure the entries are consistent in format, deadlines are met, and other questions are resolved. This person should also be the primary contact for the publisher.

COMPETITION

Is it possible to compete in the bibliography market? Yes, *if* your bibliography is unique, well-organized, available at a time when the topic is of interest, well-publicized, and as comprehensive as possible. You can obtain additional publicity if you volunteer to be a presenter or panelist on programs on which your bibliography topic will be of interest.

It is also a good idea, once you have a firm publishing commitment, to "establish your turf" by writing colleagues—potential competitors—and letting them know about your new project in as subtle a manner as possible. Your intent, of course, is to head off any potential competition.

THE FUTURE

One thing leads to another. You may decide to continue compiling bibliographies after your first experience or it may discourage you from ever producing another one. If compiling bibliographies seems to be an enjoyable occupation, pick a series of related subjects and become an expert, a specialist—someone known in the field as the authority on a particular subject. Whether or not you choose to continue producing bibliographies, the experience with the first one will stand you in good stead with all of your future writing projects. Producing bibliographies takes research skill, discipline, accuracy, attention to detail, and a good grasp of a particular subject area. They all combine to form a solid foundation for any writer.

NOTES

1. A.J. Colaianne, "The Aims and Methods of Annotated Bibliography," *Scholarly Publishing* 11 (July 1980): 330.
2. Undated letter from Mary Vance (Editor, Vance Bibliographies, Post Office Box 229, Monticello, IL 61856) to Jennifer Cargill.

SELECTED SOURCES

Bates, Marcia. "Rigorous Systematic Bibliography." *RQ* 16 (Fall 1976): 7–26.
  Describes types of bibliographies and specific principles of systematic bibliography compilation. Very helpful.
Brookes, B. C. "Jesse Shera and the Theory of Bibliography." *Journal of Librarianship* 5 (October 1973): 233–45, 258.
Bryer, Jackson R. "From Second-Class Citizenship to Respectability: The Odyssey of an Enumerative Bibliographer." *Literary Research Newsletter* 3 (1978): 55–61.
  Relates the autobiographical musings of an enumerative bibliographer, detailing some insights into the development of this type of bibliography as recognized scholarly research.
Colaianne, A. J. "The Aims and Methods of Annotated Bibliography." *Scholarly Publishing* 11 (July 1980): 321–31.
  Gives advice on the compilation of annotated bibliographies.
Evans, Martha M. "Bibliographic Control of Large Quantities of Research Materials." *RQ* 23 (Summer 1983): 393–99.
  Gives advice and practical knowledge gleaned by the author in the course of compiling an annotated bibliography. Very helpful.
Robinson, A. M. Lewin. *Systematic Bibliography: A Practical Guide to the Work of Compilation.* 3d rev. ed. Hamden, CT: Linnet Books, 1971.
  Provides practical advice to the bibliographer on the techniques needed for systematic bibliography.
Shera, Jesse H., and Egan, Margaret E. "Foundations of a Theory of Bibliography. In *Libraries and the Organization of Knowledge,* by Jesse H. Shera, pp. 18–33. Hamden, CT: Archon Books, 1965.
Wilson, Patrick. *Two Kinds of Power: An Essay on Bibliographical Control.* Berkeley, CA: University of California Press, 1968.

Writing and Publishing a Book

If you've gotten into the habit of writing fairly frequently and find it an enjoyable pastime, and if you've established a reputation as a librarian-author, you will probably decide at some point to try your hand at writing a book. If your writings have attracted some recognition, you may be contacted by a publisher or a publisher's representative to submit an idea for a book or a book idea may be suggested for your consideration. The decision to write a book, assemble a collection of essays or readings, compile a book-length bibliography, or edit the proceedings of a conference is not a decision to make lightly. You are going to have to commit a large block of time to such a project and that's only the beginning.

BIBLIOGRAPHIES

Compiling a bibliography is discussed in detail in Chapter 6. However, if and when you decide to appraoch a publisher concerning a bibliography, you will find the information in this chapter to also be helpful.

COMPILATIONS

Compiling a group of readings or essays on a certain theme is another popular publication format and one which presents its own set of special problems. If you decide to put together a collection of readings on a common topic, you must be prepared to contact the publications where the chapters or articles originally appeared and request permission from the copyright holders to reproduce those works in your book of readings. To receive permission, you may even have to negotiate a royalty agreement or provide other financial compensation to the copyright holders—or to the authors themselves.

If you decide to do a book containing essays solicited from a number of writers, you must be willing to follow several important steps in order to ensure success. First, decide on the theme and then plan the topics of the essays you intend to include in the book. The subject should be one that will produce considerable interest and hold high potential for guaranteed sales. If you can predict future trends with some accuracy and identify specific ideas and concepts that will appeal to the audience to which you are addressing the book, you can expect healthy sales, even though you won't become wealthy from the proceeds. The essays themselves must complement each other; make sure you include brief statements or outlines of what you expect to cover in each chapter.

Second, you must be able to identify potential authors for the essays. You may see yourself writing the lead essay—the one that sets the tone for the book. The other potential authors must be recognized individuals who have published and who can be expected to write reasonably well. Their individual styles should complement one another.

Third, you must contact the authors you have selected and approach them with your proposal for writing an essay for publication in your book. You may have to spend considerable time negotiating with them in order to persuade them to agree. Part of that negotiation may involve giving a share of the percentage of the royalty you expect to receive from the publisher to a particularly prominent essayist you are attempting to attract if s/he refuses to sign without some financial consideration. This practice is not as unreasonable as it sounds. After all, when the book is published with you listed as the compiler/editor, you can expect to receive the bulk of the publicity while the individual essayists will take a subordinate role. However, keep in mind that the book *was* your idea!

Once you have concluded agreements with the authors of all of the essays and have established manuscript deadlines for each of them, you will then have to be prepared to enforce those deadlines. The publisher will be looking to you to supply the finished manuscript on time, so you'll have to make certain your chapter writers don't let you down. Their essays must reach you in plenty of time for you to review them, edit them, and perhaps even return a few of them to the authors for needed rewriting. You will find it necessary to contact these essayists on a regular basis in order to gauge their progress, urge them to complete or rewrite their essays, and ensure that they meet their commitments. It is easy for an individual to agree to a flattering invitation to write an essay for a compilation that may receive favorable reviews, especially if an important person, a recognized leader in the field, is the compiler/editor who does the inviting. It is quite another thing to get these flattered writer egos to follow the necessary writing schedule and meet your deadlines. Remember, the publisher is going to hold you responsible for any delays, not your contributors. By the time you are through with a compilation, you may wish you had never had the idea in the first place. You may decide that there are easier and far more profitable ways to get a book into print with your name on the title page.

PROCEEDINGS

If you happen to find yourself as the organizational, moving force behind a conference, you may discover to your dismay that you are also responsible for gathering together those ubiquitous conference papers to publish as the official conference proceedings. Before doing anything, be sure to have a publisher committed to this project well before beginning to gather the presenters' papers, organize them, and edit them into a readable mass. Taking on such a responsibility without a formal publishing commitment could lead to disaster. Papers read at conferences or presentations made extemporaneously do not usually lend themselves to reproduction in printed form without considerable rewriting and editing. If some of the presenters talked extemporaneously, they may or may not be willing to put their thoughts into written form. Speakers who presented written papers may or may not be willing to rework their manuscript one more time so it can be considered publishable. Compiling and editing proceedings is not always a successful enterprise. There's a certain amount of risk involved. Publishers frequently resist making commitments to publish proceedings because frequently such collections do not sell well and require a great deal of expense and labor to prepare and promote.

A BOOK ON YOUR OWN

You may have a terrific idea for a book and want to write it yourself. Simply having the idea is not enough, unfortunately. You must also have both the opportunity and the determination to commit a large amount of your leisure and perhaps some of your work time to the all-consuming process of writing a book. You must plan in advance how you intend to approach your writing: by dictating it, handwriting pages and having them typed, or composing the text with a typewriter or word processor, keyboarding as you go. You may want to talk to colleagues who have written books—not compiled bibliographies or readers or edited proceedings—but those dedicated and determined souls who have actually written and labored over every word of a monograph. Find out from them precisely how much time you must be prepared to commit, the pitfalls you should anticipate and plan to avoid, and the many headaches you can expect to encounter for all your trouble.

Read some books describing the process involved in writing nonfiction and then decide if you can comply with the necessary requirements. Recall your own, earlier publications and consider the time and effort it took you to prepare those shorter works. Then consider the topic you're considering writing about.

Choosing a Topic

When you have identified a general subject area and have decided to try writing a book, just how should you approach choosing the specific topic? You may already have an idea in mind, but is it broad enough in scope and in depth to qualify as a book? Has the subject been treated before and/or was that treatment adequate? Do you already have or can you locate sufficient material? Are you willing to spend the time to do the necessary research? Is the subject a library-oriented topic? If not, do you have the specialized knowledge and expertise necessary to develop your idea into a book-length manuscript that will be recognized, appreciated, and applauded by the experts?

Before proceeding further, take some time to do a literature search. With today's database searching capabilities, you have an obvious edge, especially if you are willing to spend the money to have an extensive online search performed. The search may result in a wealth of information or a dearth of citations. If the former, you must decide if enough has already been written on the subject or if you can approach the same material with a new slant, one that will make writing a book worthwhile for both you and your intended audience. If the search produces very few relevant citations, that may be a good indication that there simply isn't enough data or information for you to use, that the topic is not broad enough in scope for a book, or that the idea is so new and unresearched that it constitutes new ground ready for you to explore.

The book idea you have in mind might also constitute appropriate material for a publication in the "how-to" category which is one of the most popular types of nonfiction works. If you want to tackle such a book, be sure you have the knowledge and experience to make it a thoroughly helpful, practical book that fills a need and is of current interest.

Once you have decided on a subject for your book, draft a rough outline of the chapters to be included in it. List as many sections within each chapter or unit as you can. Try to determine in advance the scope of both the book and of each chapter. With these concepts in mind, wait a few days and then review your outline. On second examination, is there really enough substance in your preliminary work to warrant writing a book? Be honest. If you find it lacking and don't see a way to fill in the gaps, be prepared to look for another book idea.

On the other hand, if you are encouraged enough by the results of your research to continue your project, pick a chapter at random and try researching the topic and writing a chapter draft. If random selection is too chancy for you, start with the introductory chapter. Find out just how much research you'll have to do and, at the same time, keep track of the total amount of time it takes to write your chapter. After completing the chapter, give it a few days to "cool" and then go back and revise it. Ask a knowledgeable colleague to read and comment on the content and the style. Do you still want to proceed?

Designing a Proposal

If you are still determined to continue, your next step is not to write the book but to locate a publisher willing to take on your project. Although a few publishers do prefer to see the final product or at least a draft manuscript before they will commit themselves, don't waste the energy and mental effort it takes to write a nonfiction book until you have a reasonable expectation that it will be published. Instead, first put together a formal prospectus indicating exactly what areas and topics you intend to cover in your book. This prospectus, along with a cover letter, should be sent to the publisher—usually directed to the acquisitions editor or editorial group—for review. If they are interested in the topic and in you as the potential author, they may contact you for additional information. Or they may be sufficiently impressed with your proposal or prospectus to send you a contract. Somewhere along the line, they will do a market analysis or otherwise check out the validity of the statements you've made in the prospectus, so be honest and straightforward. They will probably ask in-house staff or outside consultants to read the proposal and offer their comments.

What goes into a prospectus? It should include several key elements as illustrated in this example which may be easily modified to fit the type of book you are considering writing or compiling.

Sample Prospectus Outline

I. *Basic Description.* In this section, indicate general characteristics of the book.
  A. Theme.
  B. Format.
  C. Special features (artwork, charts, photographs, etc.).
  D. Other distinguishing features.
II. *Structure.* What will be included in the book? Give a chapter-by-chapter analysis of the anticipated contents of the book. Also, use an outline of the table of contents, annotated with one-sentence descriptions indicating what will appear in each chapter. Also indicate any additional features of the book, such as an index, an annotated bibliography, or a glossary.
III. *Responsibilities.* Who is writing the book? Is there a collaborator or are you the only author? If this is a compilation, who is responsible for the final product? If an index is included, will you supply it or would you rather the publisher arrange for a professional indexer to prepare the index (with the cost deducted from your royalties)? In what format do you propose to supply the book? Camera-ready copy? On diskettes using an agreed-to software package? What is the format of the artwork?
IV. *Market Potential.* You as the author should attempt to supply as much information as you can concerning your assessment of the potential competition and sales for this book.
  A. Potential audience. Who will be the likely purchasers? Individuals? Libraries? What types? Could your book potentially be used as a textbook or supplementary text in library schools?
  B. Competition. Are there other existing works that could be considered competitors for your work? Are there titles that appear to be competitive but which have a substantially different approach to the topic? What makes your book different or unique?
V. *Other Information.* Here you might mention whether or not the book has the potential for future revisions and future editions.
VI. *The Authors.* Provide sufficient background about yourself and the other authors, if any, indicating why you have the knowledge and skills necessary to produce such a book. A

brief biographical sketch or a copy of your resumé should be attached. Be sure to indicate any previous publications.

In summary, the prospectus should tell the publisher as much as possible about the book and why it should be written or compiled and why that publisher should contract with you to produce it.

Draft a brief cover letter to accompany the prospectus and be sure to include a telephone number where you can be reached during the day. If the publisher is interested in your prospectus, make it easy for them to contact you.

SELECTING A PUBLISHER

As you draft your prospectus, have in mind some possible publishers you might eventually send it to. Don't put together a prospectus for a bibliography and then submit it to a publisher who never publishes bibliographies. Make a quick survey of who publishes what so you'll target the right publishers. If a given publisher emphasizes an interest in certain topics, and your subject complements items on the publisher's existing list, write your prospectus with those currently in-print works in mind.

Selecting a publisher involves reviewing individual publisher catalogs or *Publishers Trade List Annual.* You should also consult *Literary Marketplace* and other directories of publishers. Look at examples of books produced by some of the publishers in which you have an interest. Are the books attractive and well-designed, quality products? Would you be proud to have your book appear with the imprint of that publisher on it? Put together a list of several potential publishers, review your prospectus, and if necessary, rewrite it and the cover letter to suit what you perceive as the proper approach to take with the publisher(s) you select as your target audience. You may submit your proposal to one potential publisher or to several. If you submit it to more than one publisher, you don't *have* to tell the editor(s) you are sending the prospectus to other publishers as well, but it is courteous to do so. They need to know that their competition also has access to your idea, and such notice may also serve to speed up the review process if your idea really appeals to them and they want to be sure to "beat out" their competitors.

The review process will probably take weeks—perhaps even months—so don't expect an immediate response to your prospectus. You may, after a period of time has passed, phone or write to ask about the status of your prospectus. If you directed your proposal to an individual, that will make it easier to contact someone who can give you an answer.

Different publishers have specific requirements or procedures they follow when considering proposals. We asked several publishers to respond to a questionnaire we compiled, and we've grouped their responses by question. Not all of the publishers responded and many of those who did respond, did so selectively.

Questionnaire

1. Publisher name and address.
2. Name and phone number of the acquisitions editor.

> **American Library Association Publishing Services.** 50 E. Huron St., Chicago, IL 60611. Respondent: Herbert Bloom.[1]
> **Greenwood Press.** 88 Post Rd., West, P.O. Box 5007, Westport, CT 06881. Respondent: Mary R. Sive.[2]
> **Knowledge Industry Publications, Inc.** 701 Westchester Ave., White Plains, NY 10604. Respondent: Susan Schwartz.[3]
> **McFarland & Company, Inc.** Box 611, Jefferson, NC 28640. Respondent: Robert Franklin.[4]
> **The Oryx Press.** 2214 N. Central at Encanto, Phoenix, AZ 85004. Respondent: Arthur H. Stickney.[5]
> **Pierian Press.** 5000 Washtenaw, Ann Arbor, MI 48104 (Send correspondence to Box 1808, Ann Arbor, MI 48106). Respondents: Tom Schultheiss, C. Edward Wall.[6]

3. Please include a sample contract and a copy of your guidelines for authors.

> **Greenwood Press:** "Author's guidelines depend on type of book."
> **McFarland & Company, Inc.:** "...we have no formal 'guidelines for authors' and, not incidentally, the majority of offerings to us are completed manuscripts."

4. Please include a brief description of your organization and its publication interests.

> **American Library Association Publishing Services:** "The works we publish are in one of two categories: works produced by ALA divisions and works produced by independent authors. In both categories the works published help librarians give improved service."
> **Greenwood Press:** "The purpose of our library publishing program may be stated as offering a vehicle for the publication of significant writings in librarianship, information sciences, and the history of computer science and to serve the profession with needed reference books. The latter include library research guides, bibliographies and bibliographic instruction tools, reference handbooks and encyclopedic dictionaries in many disciplines."
> **Knowledge Industry Publications, Inc.:** "Knowledge Industry Publications, Inc., publishes newsletters, studies, and books. The books are in four groups—The Professional Librarian, Video Bookshelf, Information and Communications Management Guides, and Communications Library. The books in The Professional Librarian Series deal primarily with technology, management, and career development for librarians. They are both practical and issues oriented."
> **McFarland & Company, Inc.:** "McFarland is a scholarly monograph, reference book, professional librarianship, and film/TV stud-

ies publisher selling largely to libraries, now doing about 50 to 55 books a year, mostly clothbound. We would like to increase the reference and professional librarianship lists."

The Oryx Press: "The Oryx Press was established in 1974. It aims its publishing and promotional activities to all library markets and selected professional audiences in health care, education, business, and other particular professional fields. The Oryx Press publishes information in various formats: print, online, microform, and soon, optical disc. Our publications include indexes, directories, bibliographies, professional guides and monographs, biographical reference works, encyclopedias, dictionaries, workbooks, handbooks, anthologies, and professional periodicals. Oryx serves the subject fields of library science, education, computer studies, nutrition, health care, gerontology, agriculture, business, and various other academic and nonacademic fields."

Pierian Press: "Pierian Press is a small, tightly-structured organization with 22 full-time and numerous part-time staff. Library and information science subjects of particular interest are technology, reference, serials and administration—areas that relate to Press journals: *Library Hi Tech, Reference Services Review,* and *Serials Review.* The Press is also a major publisher of 'library-quality' books on popular music groups and performers, e.g., The Beatles, Elvis Presley, and so on."

5. What specific advantages does an author have in publishing with your firm?

ALA: "We offer high-quality editing, design and manufacturing because our books are intended for sustained use."

Greenwood Press: "Greenwood books have an enviable record of being named 'best of the year' by various professional selection groups and of winning other awards. We offer a worldwide distribution network and enjoy strong overseas sales. Our aggressive promotion and marketing department brings our books to wide attention through the mailing of over 1 million pieces per year."

Knowledge Industry Publications, Inc.: "Knowledge Industry offers an established reputation for important library and information science publications, a proven ability to sell to the library market, and the inclusion among the company's authors of some of the most widely known leaders in the profession."

McFarland & Company, Inc.: "Personalities are likely to be important. Specific advantages would be for the author to determine...."

The Oryx Press: "In the professional fields that it serves, The Oryx Press has won a reputation for attractive, practical, significant publications. Our marketing and promotion operation is probably the most strenuous in the library field. Each book is marketed through multiple mailings, both individually with separated brochures and, when appropriate, in related subject groupings. Three million brochures were mailed to diverse groups in 1984. Real care is given to the content and appearance of each Oryx Press publication."

Pierian Press: "In many cases, the books and serials of the Press cover common areas and/or reach audiences with common interests. This provides natural opportunities to promote books and/or to highlight sections of books in journals. The journals also provide a mechanism for updating certain time-sensitive components of books. In addition to these integrated publishing practices, Pierian Press provides a general support structure that can prove particularly important to new authors."

6. What qualities do you look for in an author?

> **ALA:** "We are receptive to all librarians who wish to make a contribution through writing."
>
> **Greenwood Press:** "Intelligence, originality, ability to write, having something to say."
>
> **McFarland & Company, Inc.:** "An author should be an expert; a realist; likeable, reliable and honest; detail oriented; and a terrific writer, in that order of importance."
>
> **The Oryx Press:** "We look for authors who have: 1) a good knowledge of the information user's needs and an understanding of how information might best be organized to fit those needs; 2) attention to detail and care in execution; 3) special subject knowledge when relevant; 4) facility in writing, when applicable; 5) access to a suitable resource base; 6) resoluteness."
>
> **Pierian Press:** "Experience, discipline, enthusiasm."

7. How do you go about locating authors for titles you would like to publish? Should authors feel free to approach your representatives at professional conferences and similar gatherings or do you prefer more formal contacts?

> **ALA:** "We invite people who have been working in areas of interest to the profession. Where we have neglected to approach these individuals, we ask that they write to us. We use the ALA conferences and meetings in part for ideas and discussion."
>
> **Greenwood Press:** "Yes, by all means, many of our books originate in just that way." (In addition, Greenwood states that some authors have their initial contact with the Press as contributors to some of the Press's multivolume works. Other authors are referred to the Press by colleagues while others come to the attention of Greenwood through their published writings and conferences. Greenwood is regularly in contact with librarians, querying them concerning works they would like to see published.)
>
> **Knowledge Industry Publications:** "...feel free to approach ...representatives at professional conferences and similar gatherings." (Also, see answer to question 8.)
>
> **McFarland & Company, Inc.:** "We go about locating authors largely by opening our mail, although sometimes we pass on an idea and it's taken up. Our all-time bestseller (*Library Display Ideas*) is an example; most such editors' dream-ups are however, no better than what the transom brings."
>
> **The Oryx Press:** "We locate particular authors from their previous publications, relationship to special resource bases, or personal and professional recommendations. Potential authors, even those with very tentative ideas, are invited to approach our representatives at professional meetings or similar gatherings. We regard our consultative role in publishing matters as a reciprocal duty to the members of the profession that sustains us."
>
> **Pierian Press:** "Many authors are identified through professional contacts and recommendations. Authors are encouraged to contact the Press by phone or letter to discuss projects."

8. What do you prefer to receive from prospective authors in the way of a proposal? What points do you stress? Will you sign a contract on the basis of a proposal?

> **ALA:** "We are interested in determining from the proposal the distinctiveness and usefulness of the works we publish. We offer contracts after a sample of the author's writing is submitted."
>
> **Greenwood Press:** "Proposal should provide outline with chapter summaries, estimates of length and completion time, author's vita and samples of published writing. Contracts can be signed on basis of proposal."
>
> **Knowledge Industry Publications:** "Authors are welcome to approach Knowledge Industry by mail or in person at professional conferences. They should supply a two-page outline of the proposed book, a resume, and the answers called for in (available from publisher) Author Questionnaire. If possible, they should supply a writing sample, too."
>
> **McFarland & Company, Inc.:** "Prospective authors should so fully describe their book that we're hardly left with a question. Usually we respond 'please send' to a brief proposal if we think we're even remotely interested. We rarely consider signing a contract until we've seen at least a large sample and the length is agreed on...a large majority of our inquirers have finished, or all-but, works to offer. We admire the confidence their waiting represents and frankly have probably allowed it to be a factor in some decisions."
>
> **The Oryx Press:** "Proposals should contain: 1) a rationale/draft introduction that presents an argument for the work, its aims, and shows how it relates to other publications in the field; 2) an annotated table of contents/outline, or some other material showing how the work will be organized; 3) samples, if appropriate; 4) length estimates; 5) an estimate of the time needed to complete the work; 6) details of the intended format and method of preparation; 7) basic professional and biographical information about the author. Our consideration will center on: 1) the essential soundness of the work's substance and organization; 2) whether it will attract a sufficient audience that we can reach efficiently; 3) how it compares to other publications on the subject; 4) the likelihood of the work's projected income to counterbalance its costs of production. We do sign contracts on the basis of a satisfactory proposal."
>
> **Pierian Press:** "If an initial contact is made by phone, it should be followed by an outline and completed sample sections or chapters, whenever possible. Completed manuscripts should be submitted only after preliminary discussions have generated an expression of interest from the Press. Credentials and other publications information should be provided to the Press at the time of first contact. Contracts are occasionally signed based on preliminary contacts. More frequently, a letter of interest is issued."

9. What should prospective authors be sure to include in query letters? Proposals? What should they avoid?

> **ALA:** "There is no one matter of overriding importance."
>
> **Greenwood Press:** "Query letters should be specific, explain reason for wanting to write the book and distinguish it from existing titles. Avoid endorsements—we make our own judgment."
>
> **McFarland & Company, Inc.:** "Prospectives should consider any or

all of the following inclusions: name and return address, title of book, subject, contents, authors, their credentials, length of manuscript, its status, expected completion date, photo/illustration matters, permissions to quote or other legalistic matters, whether or not it is a multiple submission. It might help to say if the attachments should or should not be returned with any rejection (frequently it's not clear, even with those sending SASE's). One may wish to avoid a clippings file of one's hometown triumphs, a box of Kodachrome slides, vitae that exceed five typed pages, and prognostications in the hundreds of thousands of sales."

The Oryx Press: "A query letter ought to indicate the present status of the work, what the author is looking for in its publication, what the history of the work is, what its intended audience is, and why it is important. If there is no separate proposal the points touched on in question 8 ought to be included. Do not send the manuscript. We will ask for it, or parts of it, later in the reviewing process if this seems important."

10. How many proposals do you receive in a year? Of that number, how many are successful?

ALA: "We receive almost 70 proposals, with 50 being successful."
Greenwood Press: "We have seven acquisitions editors and have never taken a survey of number of proposals received."
Knowledge Industry Publications, Inc.: (See question 8.)
McFarland & Company, Inc.: "We get about 10 offers a week and accept about one of them. Slightly fewer than that are successful."
The Oryx Press: "We received approximately 350 proposals during the past year and signed some 40 contracts."
Pierian Press: "We have never kept track of the number of proposals received in a year—perhaps 100 or so. Between 20 percent and 25 percent end up as Pierian Press books."

11. What is your average turnaround time in response to proposals and manuscript submissions?

ALA: "Three weeks for proposals, five weeks for manuscripts."
Greenwood Press: "Two to four weeks."
Knowledge Industry Publications, Inc.: "Two to four weeks."
McFarland & Company, Inc.: "We turn around 95 percent of proposals and submissions in three days. The other five percent take a week, say, up, to six weeks, to our embarrassment."
The Oryx Press: "From receipt of a proposal to conclusion of a review will take, on average, from six to 20 weeks. In the lengthier reviews this time often is spent in adjusting or altering the proposal."
Pierian Press: "Thirty to 45 days."

12. Some publishers typeset copy while others require the author to provide camera-ready copy. Which do you prefer and why? Are there specific advantages/disadvantages for the author?

ALA: "We take both, with preference governed by the financial considerations attached to the project."
Greenwood Press: "Typesetting vs. camera-ready depends on type of book. We do both and offer authors an improved royalty rate

for providing camera-ready copy."

Knowledge Industry Publications, Inc.: "Knowledge Industry requires double-spaced, typed manuscript. Receiving the material in this form allows the editorial staff, in consultation with the author, to polish the presentation before it is typeset."

McFarland & Company, Inc.: "We typeset and prefer it, currently, but have no objection to certain works being provided camera-ready by knowledgeable authors. Frequently the correspondence, corrections, and calendric uncertainties militate against author camera copy. Then there's the matter of recompensing them for this additional labor—since they're usually not experts, they'll be overpaid unless one insults them or demands it free. Furthermore, the books may not look quite as nice as they would if typeset or be as economically laid out."

The Oryx Press: "Most of our present books are typeset, but we will consider camera-ready copy in special cases. The advantages for the author are minimal work in physically preparing the manuscript and an attractive published work which has better sales appeal. The disadvantage is that the process can be costly and time-consuming."

Pierian Press: "Pierian Press typesets books in most cases."

13. More and more authors are using word processors. Do you have restrictions on the quality of typed copy submitted for publication? Will you accept manuscripts submitted on floppy disks? Are you capable of downloading copy direct to your computer?

ALA: "We take disks with the printed form prepared on a letter-quality printer."

Greenwood Press: "We provide manuscript typing paper and instructions."

Knowledge Industry Publications, Inc.: "Typed copy must be double-spaced, and the print quality must be good enough to allow for easy reading and photocopying. The ink must be black. Letter-quality printing from a word processor, rather than dot matrix printing, is greatly preferred. (There is, of course, no requirement that a word processor be used. A typewriter is fine.) Knowledge Industry does not at this time accept manuscripts on floppy disks, nor is downloading possible."

McFarland & Company, Inc.: "We're not quite ready for accepting floppies but are moving close in many ways. We have a large computerized typesetting system newly in place. (It will probably be quite a while before we'd want proposals on disks, however.) The disadvantages are similar to those with author-provided camera copy: minute miscommunications can end all."

The Oryx Press: "All manuscripts (from a word processor or a typewriter) should be double-spaced, on consecutively numbered pages, with 1½-inch margins all around. We encourage the submission of manuscripts on floppy disk, using agreed-upon word processing software if possible. We can download (or upload) from IBM-compatible disk or 1600 BPI ASCII format tape. We also take non-IBM-compatible diskettes and convert them, where possible."

Pierian Press: "If manuscript copy is submitted in paper format, copy should conform to the following format: double-spaced, wide margins, fully-formed character output. Pierian Press can accept manuscripts formatted for the IBM PC, PC/XT or PC/AT. Copy can also be accepted on nine-track tape for computer manipulation on a Hewlett-Packard main-frame computer: copy can be transmitted electronically. Please enquire for specific details."

14. What do you offer prospective authors in the way of contract terms including royalties?

> **ALA:** "We offer advances and competitive royalties."
> **Greenwood Press:** "Terms vary according to type of book."
> **Knowledge Industry Publications, Inc.:** "Standard royalties."
> **McFarland & Company, Inc.:** "The royalty figures are frequently 10 percent and 12Apercent."
> **The Oryx Press:** "Our royalty rates rival those of other publishers. These are not publicly divulged."
> **Pierian Press:** "Royalty terms vary slightly depending on type of book—trade versus library book, and whether part of a series or not. Library books (not part of a series) generally receive 10 percent of net sales for the first 1,000 copies, 15 percent of net sales thereafter."

15. What can a prospective author expect in the way of promotional services?

> **ALA:** "Authors may expect intensive initial promotion and sustained promotion thereafter to appropriate audiences."
> **Greenwood Press:** (See question 5.) "Promotion welcomes authors' suggestions for reviewing media, bulk sales, special mailings, etc., and follows them up."
> **Knowledge Industry Publications, Inc.:** "Promotional mailings of the entire Professional Librarian line are done several times a year. For 1985 there will probably be five such mailings. In addition, appropriate books are displayed at conventions of such organizations as the American Society for Information Science and ALA. Press releases are sent out for each book published."
> **McFarland & Company, Inc.:** "Our approach to promotion is probably similar to our peers: two or more mass catalog mail-outs a year, seasonal or subject brochures bulkmailed, flyers selectively mailed and supplied author; very generous review copy send-outs and followups; judicious ad space in major library periodicals; scrupulous attention to appearance on databases, national and international listings; ABI and BIP (and similar) cooperation; LC cooperation, library conference exposure, close wholesaler/jobber communications (e.g., Baker & Taylor's *Directions*), special exhibits, and so on. Keeping the books promoted and for sale many years is as important as any factor above."
> **The Oryx Press:** "Advance press announcements go to a wide range of potentially interested individuals, groups, and publicity sources. An individual advertising piece for each title is mailed to a variety of potential customers (usually with other related mailing pieces), normally in repeated mailings. Book review copies are distributed. We exhibit at a large number of professional meetings."
> **Pierian Press:** "Books are promoted through Press journals, other journals and direct mail."

16. What advice would you offer an author with proposal in hand? Is there a specific approach that will get your attention?

> **ALA:** "The signal we like is that a work is shown to help librarians serve their public better or operate more efficiently in their organizations. The need for the work must be clear."
>
> **Greenwood Press:** "Write or call me. I am interested in new ideas and respond to all inquiries quickly."
>
> **McFarland & Company, Inc.:** "Our advice is to come on very brief and business-like in your initial inquiry, showing a real feel not only for your subject but its market, yet not omitting to completely describe your work (as opposed merely to stating and defending its topic). Knowing of, and mentioning, significant existing competitive works is a plus!"
>
> **The Oryx Press:** "No unusual approach is needed to gain our attention. We read all of our mail. A carefully prepared and well-considered prospectus is the surest way to get quick action from us."
>
> **Pierian Press:** "Call and speak to an editor. Succinctly describe the project, and provide an indication of personal credentials. Be prepared to follow-up immediately with written materials in greater depth, covering the same topics."

Not all publishers queried responded and some who did, did not respond to all questions asked. Others responded with the precondition that they not be directly quoted or that they wanted to edit the responses included in this text. Publishing is a competitive business, after all, and publishers want to keep their game plans secret. Some publishers supplied information that could be used in a general way in the text itself.

COLLABORATION

Another decision you must make before beginning to write your book is whether to work with one or more collaborators, with each author agreeing to provide an equal part, or specified portion, of the finished product. There are both advantages and disadvantages to collaboration. In deciding to work with a collaborator, consider these points.

- Does s/he complement your talents? For example, does one of you like to do the basic research while the other prefer to pull together the data?
- Do you have similar work habits and work habits that each can tolerate in the other?
- Can you work out an agreement up front, stipulating who is responsible for what aspect of the finished product?
- Are you able to meld your respective writing skills so that the reader is unaware of a change in authorship from chapter to

chapter? This task can often be accomplished by scrupulous editing and reediting of each other's writing.

- Can you both maintain a good rapport, no matter what the pressures and problems may be?
- Do you understand the distractions that may affect each of you during the course of the joint project: family, hobbies, workload, tragedies, unexpected events.
- If you are working at a distance, can you each establish and maintain a work schedule, and exchange drafts on a regular basis? Can you maintain regular correspondence or phone contact?
- Have you worked together before?
- Are you able to arrange regular meetings for extended work sessions?
- Can you decide who will receive top billing on the title page without later recriminations?
- Can you agree to support each other if disagreements arise between one of you and the publisher or your in-house editor?
- Can you effectively combat petty jealousy and offset demands from friends and family who may attempt to disrupt the working relationship?

If you are beginning to think that collaboration isn't easy, you are correct. It certainly isn't a good choice for everyone. Before initiating such a relationship for the first time, be sure you know your potential partner as well as possible. Ask colleagues who have collaborated on books exactly what pitfalls to avoid—or to anticipate, and be prepared to take their advice.

CONTRACTS, COPYRIGHT, ROYALTIES, ADVANCE PAYMENTS, RIGHTS AND PERMISSIONS

There are always legal considerations involved in writing a book. Once you have passed the hurdles of submitting a prospectus, having it reviewed and accepted and have reached agreement with the publisher, you must now deal with binding legal documents. Usually it isn't necessary to consult a lawyer, but you may want to talk to colleagues who have gone through this kind of contractual process. Publishers are usually honest people and their legal documents have been drawn up carefully. However, it is to your advantage to read each line and give careful consideration to what you are being asked to sign. The documents were drawn up carefully—but they were designed primarily to protect the publisher.

Contracts

When the publisher has accepted your proposal, a contract will be sent to you to sign. Usually you will be sent multiple copies to sign and return to the publisher for his/her signature. A completed copy will then be returned to you for your files. In addition to signing the contract, you may also have to make decisions concerning several other legal aspects of publishing your book.

- Who retains the copyright? If you want it, indicate your name in the appropriate space.
- What is the completion date? Be reasonable and don't cut the time too short—or give yourself an excessive amount of time.

Though the publisher provides the contract, you can probably amend it slightly, with the agreement of the publisher. But don't be unreasonable. If the publisher states that you must submit the manuscript typed and double-spaced, don't insist on submitting it on microcomputer diskettes.

A contract is a two-way agreement: Both parties must live up to its terms and conditions. If an amendment in the terms is necessary (for example, an extension on the completed manuscript due date becomes necessary), request the change in writing and ask that the response be supplied to you in writing.

Copyright

The publisher may state in the contract that the copyright remains in the publisher's name. You should consider very seriously retaining the copyright in your name. Then, when the book has gone out of print, you won't have to request permission to use all or part of the text in another book. If you have created a consulting firm or other business to which your royalties, consulting fees, etc. are channeled, you may want the copyright to be listed under the name of that partnership or corporation.

Royalties

Royalties are payments to authors based upon a percentage of the sales of the book and are usually paid once or twice yearly by the publisher. The publisher may pay your royalties based on the net sales from November through April, but the actual payment may not be sent to you until the end of the following June. The royalty may be paid on the basis of actual paid sales or on sales that have been made even if the money hasn't actually been collected. The individual policy of each publisher will determine when you are paid and on what basis. Your contract will clearly state what your royalty percentage is and how you will receive it. The royalty percentage may vary based on the number of books sold or according to whether the sales are domestic or foreign.

Don't expect a book in the library or information science field or a reference book to even approach the sales figures of a trade publication. One to two thousand copies sold for each title is considered an acceptable return on investment.

Sample Contract

Following is a sample contract from an established publisher. Other publishers' contracts will be similar.

AGREEMENT made this _____ day of _____, 19____, between
(Name of Publisher) and

Author: _____

Author: _____

Author: _____

(hereinafter, and if there is more than one author, then all of them
collectively, called "the Author;" and (Name of Publisher), hereinafter
called "the Publisher").

1   RIGHTS   The Author hereby grants and assigns to the Publisher
    GRANTED   for the full term of copyright the exclusive right to
                publish and vend in all languages throughout the world the
                Work provisionally entitled

                (hereinafter called the "Work"). The Publisher shall have
                the sole right to publish, license, or otherwise exploit
                the Work in all forms and in all media, including, without
                limitation, hardbound and paperbound book publication,
                serial, translation, computer-based services, and all
                other rights appertaining to the Work.

2   COPYRIGHT   The Publisher shall copyright said work in the name of
                (Name of Publisher or Author(s)) in the United States, and
                elsewhere as the Publisher may elect, and may renew such
                copyright to the extent permitted by law.

3   MANUSCRIPT The Author will deliver to the Publisher before
                _____, 19_____, either A) a
                manuscript for the Work, in form and substance
                satisfactory to the Publisher, or B) a manuscript for the
                Work which shall consist of: a hard copy printout, and
                after copy editing and marking of the printout with
                typesetting codes, 5 1/2" floppy disks upon which the said
                copy revisions and typesetting codes have been put, in
                form and substance satisfactory to the Publisher. At the
                same time the Author shall deliver to the Publisher all
                necessary auxiliary materials, and all permissions to use
                copyrighted material. The Author shall retain a copy of
                the manuscript and auxiliary materials and will read and
                correct all proofs.

The Publisher may make the manuscript conform to such style and punctuation, spelling, capitalization, and usage as the Publisher deems appropriate.

Except as may be provided elsewhere in this Agreement, the Author is solely responsible for requesting and securing, as necessary or required, all final and complete copyright and other proprietary rights, licenses, permissions, or releases from the owners or holders of such rights, at no cost or expense to the Publisher. The written evidence and record of all transactions, negotiations, and agreements concerning the requesting and receiving of all necessary and required permissions will be maintained in good order by the Author, and transmitted, in complete form, to the Publisher, prior to the actual setting of type for the Work. Except as may be provided elsewhere in the Agreement, the Author is solely responsible for providing, at no cost or expense to the Publisher, suitable camera-ready maps, photographs, and other illustrations selected for inclusion, and approved by the Publisher

If the Author fails to deliver the complete material within the specified time, the Publisher may decline to publish the Work and recover any and all amounts which may have been advanced to the Author.

AUTHOR ALTERATIONS

If the Author fails to deliver to the Publisher any items necessary to the completion of the manuscript, or if the manuscript does not conform to specifications, the Publisher shall have, in addition to its other remedies, but without limitation as to remedies, the option to supply the items necessary to the completion or conformity to specifications of the manuscript and/or to rewrite or to compile anew the manuscript and charge and offset related costs against any sums accruing to the Author, such offset to be against the first payments due to Author until paid in full. The expense of Author's alterations, exclusive of printer's errors, made in proof in excess of 10% of the cost of composition shall be chargeable against the Author and shall be deducted from any sums due the Author under this Agreement.

4   COMPETITIVE WORKS

During the term of this Agreement the Author shall not publish or permit the publication of any material written in whole or in part by the author that is derived from or competitive to the Work or the rights herein granted without the prior written consent of the Publisher.

5   REVISED OR SUBSEQUENT EDITIONS

The Author agrees to revise the first and subsequent editions of the Work at the request of the Publisher and to supply any new matter necessary from time to time to keep the said Work up to date. The Author shall deliver the final revised manuscript in form and content satisfactory to the Publisher within a reasonable period of time. Unless otherwise agreed, provisions of this agreement shall apply with respect to the revised edition except for royalty computations which will treat the revised edition as a new work.

6   PUBLICATION OF THE WORK

All decisions and details as to the publication, as well as to the style, illustrations, time and manner of production, of price, publication and advertisement and the number and distribution of free copies shall be left to the sole discretion of the Publisher, who shall bear all expenses of production, publication, and advertisement.

AUTHOR'S COPIES

The Publisher shall furnish the Author, free of charge, 4 copies of the Work as published; and any additional copies desired by the Author for his/her personal use shall be supplied at a discount of 50% from list price, without royalty to the Author.

7   ROYALTY   The Publisher shall pay to the Author as full compensation for all services on the following basis:

     a.   Publication in book form:
        (1) Domestic Sales:

        (2) Foreign Sales:

     b.   Licenses: in the event the Work is licensed, the net amounts received by the Publisher therefrom shall be divided equally between the parties hereto in lieu of royalty, less direct expenses.

     c.   The Author's royalty account with the Publisher shall be deemed a single consolidated account to embrace any publication agreement with the Publisher, and all charges and credits provided for in this or any other agreement between the Author and the Publisher shall be made against said account.

       DIVISION OF   If there be more than one author, any monies payable to
       ROYALTIES   them shall be divided among them in the following proportions:

8   **ROYALTY**   Statements of account shall be rendered on each 6/30 and
      PAYMENTS   12/31 covering the six months' periods ended the preceding 4/30 and 10/31, respectively, and shall be accompanied by payments in full of the net amount shown thereon to the Author's credit

                     In any case where the Work has not earned the amount of any advance or the Author has received an overpayment of royalties or is otherwise indebted to the Publisher, the Publisher may deduct the amount of such unearned advance, overpayment or royalty or other indebtedness from any amount due the Author.

                     Any advances which the Publisher may have made to the Author prior to acceptance of the completed manuscript as provided in Paragraph 3 above shall be repaid to the Publisher promptly if the Publisher determines in good faith that such manuscript and auxiliary materials are not satisfactory and returns them to the Author.

9   OUT OF PRINT   In the event that the Work goes out of print or is not available in any other form from the Publisher and the Author is not indebted to the Publisher, the Author may demand that the Publisher place the Work in print and unless the Publisher shall do so or make satisfactory arrangements for reprinting the Work within six months, the Publisher shall re-convey and re-assign to the Author all rights hereunder except that the Author shall not be released from any of his/her obligations under Paragraph 11 below.

                     The Author shall have the right to purchase from the Publisher at cost any existing plates of the Work or other reproductive media or material, and any existing sheet and bound stock which are the unrestricted property of the Publisher. If the Author shall not take over the said plates or other reproductive media or material or existing sheets and bound stock, and pay for the same within thirty days following written notification by the Publisher, the Publisher may destroy said plates and sell all copies or sheets then on hand at such prices as it can obtain.

10   FORCE   The Work shall not be deemed out of print nor shall the
      MAJEURE   Publisher be liable because of delays caused by wars, civil riots, strikes, fires, acts of God, governmental restrictions or because of similar or dissimilar circumstances beyond its control.

11   WARRANTY   The Author warrants and represents that he/she is the sole owner of the Work and all the rights herein granted and has full right and power to make this agreement; that the Work is not a violation of any copyright, proprietary or personal right; that the Author has not in any manner granted, assigned, encumbered or disposed of any of the rights herein granted to the Publisher or any rights adverse to or inconsistent therewith; nor are there any rights outstanding which would diminish, encumber, or impair the full enjoyment or exercise of the right herein granted the Publisher; that no part of the Work is libelous, obscene or unlawful, or violates any right of privacy. The Author agrees to hold harmless and indemnify the Publisher and all others claiming under it against all damages suffered and expenses incurred based on the breach of such representation or warranty.

In the event of any claim against the Publisher based in whole or in part on allegations which, if proved, would constitute a breach of any of the above representations and warranties, the Publisher shall have the right to defend the same through counsel of its own choosing. The Author shall cooperate with the Publisher in defending the claim and shall provide all information and documents required by the Publisher's counsel. The Author shall indemnify and hold harmless the Publisher, licensees from the Publisher, and any seller of the Work from any and all liability, damages, and expenses, including without limitation reasonable attorneys' fees resulting from or connected with such claim.

12   RETURN OF   The Publisher shall take all suitable measures for the
      THE AUTHOR'S preservation of the Author's manuscript and illustrative
      MANUSCRIPT   materials, if any, supplied by the Author; but, except for
      & ORIGINAL   acts of gross negligence by the Publisher, the Publisher
      MATERIALS   shall not be responsible for their loss or damage. If the Author does not request the return of the original manuscript and illustrative materials within twelve months from the date of initial publication of the Work, all such materials shall become property of the Publisher to be kept or disposed of, free from any claim on the part of the Author.

13   SPECIAL   1) The cost of indexing shall be considered as an advance
      PROVISIONS   against royalties.

14   BINDING   This Agreement shall be binding upon and inure to the
      EFFECT   benefit of the parties hereto, the heirs and personal representatives of the Author, and the successors and assigns of the Publisher. The Author may assign only his/her right to receive any amounts which become payable after receipt by the Publisher of notice of such assignment. The Publisher may assign this Agreement or any interest therein.

15   MISCEL-   This Agreement has been executed in the State of _____
      LANEOUS   and shall be governed by and construed in accordance with the laws thereof.

The marginal captions are inserted for convenient reference only and are not a part of this Agreement.

This Agreement constitutes the total and entire agreement between the parties and supersedes any other written or oral statements concerning publication of the Work.

IN WITNESS WHEREOF, the parties have duly executed this Agreement as of the date first written.

(Name of Publisher)

By:_____
    President

```
Author_____
Residence Address_____
City, State, Zip Code_____
Social Security Number_____
Telephone Number (home)_____(work)_____
Author_____
Residence Address_____
City, State, Zip Code_____
Social Security Number_____
Telephone Number (home)_____(work)_____
Author_____
Residence Address_____
City, State, Zip Code_____
Social Security Number_____
Telephone Number (home)_____(work)_____
```

Advance Payments

A publisher may provide advance payments for manuscript typing, special artwork, or similar special needs. These advance payments will be recorded and eventually deducted from your initial royalties. You will probably not receive a penny of your profits until this advance payment has been repaid. If at all possible, try to avoid requesting an advance payment. If you are part of an organization, such as an academic institution, that encourages your publishing activities, it may even be willing to provide necessary typing assistance or offer you a grant to subsidize that expenditure.

Rights and Permissions

When you intend to reproduce material supplied by others, such as a form or document, you'll need to secure permission to reprint that material in your book. Your publisher should supply forms for this purpose. You may also find that a letter of agreement between the author and the copyright holder will serve as a substitute.

WRITING THE BOOK

The proposal has been accepted. The contract is signed. Any agreements of collaboration have been resolved. All you have to do now is write the book. Right? Well...

Not so fast. Don't assume that you will just get the book written or compiled by your 12- to 18-month deadline. Some considerable effort on your part must go into planning if you are going to operate your writing project according to a schedule.

Research

Plan how much time you will need to conduct any necessary research. Allow time for travel (if that will be necessary), completion of interlibrary loan requests, responses from questionnaires, or other time-consuming tasks that must be completed before you can proceed.

Organization

Allow time to organize your notes, put your work space in order, and complete any pressing or unfinished tasks that will distract from the writing effort later if you don't resolve them in the beginning.

Scheduling

Identify blocks of time when you know you can write on a regular, scheduled basis. Design a writing timetable you can stick with and establish reasonable goals relating to the amount of work to be accomplished in each session.

Set some intermediate goals. For example, if the completed product is to be delivered to the publisher by a certain date, plan when you will have one-quarter completed, one-half, three-fourths, etc. Decide when you will have the all-but-final draft of the completed manuscript ready for your final revision. As you work, each chapter will go through several drafts. Establish a point at which you will set aside each chapter, for example, the fourth draft, and move on to the next chapter; do initial drafts of all chapters; and then revise each one as needed. It is a good idea to take your outline of the book and break it down into several time segments with deadlines attached to each. Why all the interest in goals and deadlines? So you'll stay on schedule, finish on time, and live up to your contractual obligations. If you don't build in little time segments with appropriate reminders, you could easily fall behind schedule without knowing it and then have to work at a fever pitch to catch up.

Allow some "cushion" time for you to have the final draft in hand and ready to go to the publisher. This "cushion" allows time to accommodate last-minute problems, such as late-arriving artwork, a sick typist, or delays in receiving vital permissions.

Gauging Progress

In order to stick with your project, you must have positive reinforcement to assure yourself that you are accomplishing something. You need to "see" examples of progress to keep from becoming discouraged. One effective way to provide this is to place each completed page in a large, three-ring notebook, separating each chapter with dividers. As you complete a draft of each chapter, you will begin to see the results of your mental and physical labor take shape and will begin to feel that wonderful sense of accomplishment. The dividers can also serve as a place to write or attach reminder notes about further revisions needed or you can simply attach your revisions directly to these pages. The dividers can be used to indicate the target dates for completion of each revision or your status report on each chapter.

These notebooks are easy to transport and can fit into a briefcase or be carried with you so you can revise or rewrite at any time—during coffee breaks, at lunch, while waiting for an appointment, in an airport terminal. Always keep the latest revision in the notebook; previous versions, if you elect to retain them, should be stored.

Self-Discipline

This is going to be an important consideration if you are going to meet your deadline. If it is absent, you will have endless delays and may never complete your book. If you are weak in the self-discipline department, a book-length project may not be in your best interest. Be ready to use all the tricks you have developed over the years to keep yourself meeting deadlines and working on the project.

Special Elements

Depending upon your subject and its arrangement, you may find it necessary/worthwhile to include some special effects which may take the form of charts or graphs, photographs, or artwork. These elements should be included only if your publisher and editor are aware of their inclusion and only if it is clearly understood in what form they will be submitted, how many are to be included, and that their inclusion is necessary and contributes to the content and eventual success of the book. Artwork adds to the cost of the book and publishers produce their books on a carefully prepared budget. Don't suddenly surprise your editor with previously unmentioned special effects.

Graphics and Artwork

If you use graphs, charts, or other media, be sure they are either professionally produced or are presented in such a way that the publisher's art department can replicate them easily and accurately. Be sure to indicate where they must appear in the book and make sure you include proper references to them within the text.

If you use drawings, cartoons, photographs, or other artwork, either provide professionally produced copy yourself or be sure you have an agreement that the publisher's art department or a contract artist will produce them. The cost may be deducted from your royalties, so don't be surprised if that happens.

As we've said, artwork, especially that which must be produced by the publisher, adds to the cost of the book and may reduce profits, or more likely, add to the sale price of your book. Special, expensive processing or printing may be necessary; this not only takes money but also requires extra time in the production schedule, especially if the publisher's staff has already designed the book, without knowing anything about the artwork you plan to submit. When you consider artwork, review these points:

- Is the effect worth the additional expense?
- Does it enhance the manuscript?
- Does it contribute significantly to the content?
- Can you do without it and still produce an acceptable manuscript?

Indexing

If your manuscript calls for an index, you can do the indexing yourself or a professional indexer can be hired. If a professional indexer is hired, either you may contract and pay for his/her services or the publisher may arrange for indexing to be done with the understanding that charges will be deducted from—you guessed it—your royalties. This arrangement should be detailed in your contract. If you feel confident and have the time for a very detail-oriented task, go ahead and index it yourself. However, you should consult manuals and experienced colleagues before you undertake such a chore. If you've never done any indexing, it is preferable to hire a professional indexer, trained to perform the procedure efficiently and effectively, to do the work. Why?

- Professional indexers are skilled in their trade and have established procedures and time-tested techniques to follow. They will take a fresh approach to your manuscript and will do the job quickly and accurately.
- This is a time-consuming task and, coming as it does at the end of your writing activity, you may not be mentally suited to tackle it.

PRODUCING THE FINAL PRODUCT

The final manuscript to be sent to the publisher should be as complete as you can make it. Quotations and facts should be double-checked for accuracy. Charts and columns of figures should be reexamined. Locations of special inserts should be carefully noted. Citations should be correct. The manuscript should be revised carefully with attention paid to grammar, structure, word flow, and content. This doesn't mean that the editor to whom you've been assigned won't still have questions or requests for rewrites, but that shouldn't stop you from attempting to achieve perfection.

Supply the required number of manuscript copies, in the requested format, as specified in your contract. If one-inch margins on all sides are specified, comply. If black ink is required, meet the requirement. Don't take shortcuts at the last minute. Do it correctly even if it means calling the editor and asking for a couple of extra days to put things in order.

If you finish well ahead of the deadline, you may want to take advantage of the cheaper postal rates provided by the U.S. Postal Service for shipment of manuscripts. However, for peace of mind, it is probably a better idea for you to splurge and ship it by first class or an express mail, or use an insured carrier such as United Parcel Service or Federal Express. They will assure you of faster delivery, and you'll have fewer moments of anxiety. Use a service that provides insurance *and* a receipt. You need documentation of proof that your shipment arrived safely. Be sure to get it. Also, be sure to keep a complete copy of whatever it is you have submitted.

Prior to or right after shipping the completed manuscript, call your editor and inform him/her that your book is on its way. Ask him/her to drop you a card when it arrives if your method of shipment does not provide delivery confirmation service.

At this point, you may be tempted, after all these months of hard labor, to treat yourself to a vacation. If you do so, notify your editor that you will be unavailable for consultation for a period of time while s/he is beginning to work on the manuscript. Or, at least leave word where you can be reached if questions arise.

ESTABLISHING RAPPORT

At some point in your relationship with the publisher, an editor will be assigned to your project. Do what you can to get to know that editor. From the time you sign the contract, you should let your publisher know—and especially after an editor is assigned—where you are in the production of the manuscript. Keep the editor informed about any snags you encounter.

Try to establish a good working relationship with your editor. S/he will receive the completed manuscript and will be the one person who asks you to clarify passages, do rewrites, respond to comments on content, and read and approve proofs. This individual is your primary publisher contact. The two of you may never meet, but you'll certainly correspond and talk on the phone or via electronic mail. If you produce additional books for this same publisher in the future, that same editor could be assigned to you again, assuming that you are able to establish a good working relationship. Your editor is also the contact who can put you in touch with other personnel within the company, such as the marketing people, and assist you in building a solid author/publisher working relationship.

Don't be dismayed if you find that you cannot establish a friendly relationship with everyone within the company. There are always a few unpleasant people everywhere. Concentrate on those with whom you can work well and concentrate on making your experience with your publisher a pleasant one.

MARKETING YOUR BOOK

The publisher's marketing department will probably contact you for suggestions on potential sales markets, review sources, and target groups for mass mailings. Be prepared to provide whatever assistance you can. Suggest periodicals that you know will reach your audience, periodicals in which advertisements or reviews might appear. Don't be shy in suggesting specific targets for any mass mailings the publisher may intend to send out.

If the publisher's marketing department doesn't contact you, make your suggestions anyway. They can ignore them if they choose, but you know the audience for which you have written the book better than anyone. If you will be appearing at a conference or making a presentation, let your editor and/or the marketing department know about it, especially if your presentation will be relevant to the book you have just completed. Indicate your willingness to be available in their exhibit booth at the conference and your willingness to greet visitors.

SELF-PUBLISHING

Are you a risk taker? An urge to become part of our free enterprise system is not the best or even a good reason to try self-publishing.

Have you tried every avenue available for the publication of your book? Perhaps the publishers have a good reason to not be interested? Is your potential market so limited? Or is the competition intense?

You'll read marvelous success stories about self-publishers who succeeded. However, there are far more horror stories about the people who didn't. Do lots of research before you decide to publish a book yourself. It's true that there are some success stories, so try to talk to some of those people if possible and attempt to find out all of the advantages and the disadvantages. One advantage is that all of the profits—if any—will be yours, rather than just a percentage. But you may also wind up with a garage or attic full of unsold books and astronomical printer and bindery bills to pay. Some self-publishing points to consider are these:

- Are you so determined to get your work in print that self-publishing is the only route left to you?
- Are you so committed to your book that you are willing to invest your savings in the project?
- Can you handle all of the elements necessary to get your work into print?
- Can you devise marketing strategy?
- Can you negotiate a printing contract?
- Can you write a budget for the entire project and live with it?
- Can you commit yourself to providing the funding, either from your savings or from an agreeable banker?
- Do you have the talent and fiscal resources to follow through on production?

SUMMARY

Writing or compiling a book is difficult, painstaking work. It means giving up extraordinary amounts of time. The monetary payoff for a nonfiction book in the library and information field is not great. If you take your first royalty check and divided it by the hours you worked on the book, you will find that you have been working for pennies.

Self-discipline is a must. You have to set your own deadlines and those of your coauthors or contributors. You must have a driving commitment to complete the task, and a task it will become by the time you are through.

You must take special care in locating the right publisher. You've got to establish an effective working relationship with the publisher, your editor, and any other people involved in the project. You must pay attention to detail, try to avoid surprises both for yourself and your publisher, and keep your nose to the grindstone for months on end. It takes courage, money, time, and mental commitments, as well as talent. But, once you are through and you hold the finished, bound book in your hand or see it on display at a conference, you'll know it was all worthwhile. And you will probably be thinking of your next book if you aren't already writing it.

NOTES

1. Correspondence from Herbert Bloom, ALA, undated (1985), to Brian Alley.

2. Correspondence from Mary R. Sive, Greenwood Press, January 23, 1985, to Brian Alley.

3. Correspondence from Susan Schwartz, Knowledge Industry Publications, Inc., undated (1985), to Brian Alley.

4. Correspondence from Robert Franklin, McFarland & Company, Inc., January 15, 1985, to Brian Alley.

5. Correspondence from Arthur H. Stickney, The Oryx Press, March 18, 1985, to Brian Alley and Jennifer Cargill.

6. Correspondence from Tom Schultheiss and C. Edward Wall, Pierian Press, undated (1985), to Brian Alley.

Part III
Writing and Editing for Career Advancement

Editing Newsletters and Periodicals

One of the best ways to become active in the professional writing arena is through involvement as a publications editor. If you are thinking that editors have to possess a variety of writing skills that you couldn't possibly hope to attain with your limited background, remember that you have plenty of time to acquire them. You shouldn't even try to start at or even near the top. Instead, begin with relatively basic, simple editing chores and progress from there.

EDITING NEWSLETTERS

Newsletters come in all sizes and shapes and cover a variety of subjects. Depending upon the size of your library, you may have a library newsletter devoted to the internal goings-on of your own organization. Such so-called house organs reflect the activity of the staff and promote new policies; some of the more sophisticated publications may even offer guest editorials expounding a particular viewpoint on an issue of interest to the staff. Pretty dull stuff, you say? Possibly, but nevertheless a great training ground for would-be editors and newsletter publishers.

If the material included in each newsletter issue is worthy of being printed and distributed, it is certainly worth shaping into quality, readable form. That is where your talent as a volunteer editor can come in, so whenever an editorial vacancy comes along, volunteer. Editing is often time-consuming, difficult work and, as a result, it should be easy to locate opportunities if you let it be known that you are available. Maybe you haven't had any direct experience editing newsletters but, if you are interested in learning and like to write, you can learn what you need to know in a relatively short amount of time. There are a number of good books on the subject (see the bibliography at the end of this book). The more serious and determined you are, the better job you'll do. And like anything else, the more you do it, the better you'll get and the sooner you'll find yourself being offered more responsible assignments.

Getting Started

Opportunity is the first thing you'll need. Volunteering for editorial assignments through professional organizations is one way to obtain an editorial position. If you are the least bit active in state, regional, and even national library organizations, you'll learn of editorial vacancies as they arise. If there's nothing available at the time you happen to be looking, volunteer to help in any capacity. Most organizational newsletters have a regular and ongoing shortage of talent of all kinds and welcome volunteers. A letter to an editor will often produce that first assignment. Most newsletter editing (certainly the house organ variety) is unpaid and depends entirely on the assistance of volunteers who do everything from writing and editing to printing and mailing. Somewhere in that collection of activities is a job for you, but you won't know until you ask.

Duties and Responsibilities

Some newsletters are one-person operations with the editor/writer/publisher doing everything. That's not necessarily what you are looking for unless the former "one person" is willing and able to stay on for a period of time while you learn the ropes. In most cases, you'll probably want to avoid the do-it-all-yourself approach. A newsletter with several staffers offers a division of labor arrangement under which you, as the new volunteer, can both learn and contribute to gradually over time.

Once you grasp the goals and objectives of the newsletter, you'll be in a good position to accept a variety of assignments. So be prepared and be willing to fly by the seat of your pants as you learn on the job. There will be such disparate assignments as writing an editorial, editing a feature article, rewriting a poorly written, but much-needed article, and editing a regular column. Don't forget the book reviews. Lots of newsletters include them, and someone has to write them.

Soliciting articles, guest editorials, opinion pieces, features, and interviews is a big part of an editor's job. Contrary to what you might think, editors frequently have to find the people to do the writing and then coax, cajole, threaten, and plead with them to produce copy and meet those unyielding deadlines. If you are that serious and determined person we spoke of earlier and you become accomplished in the art of motivating writers, you'll soon find that your value as an editor increases dramatically.

Occasionally, editors are called upon to rewrite a submission which might otherwise be rejected. That's where your writing skills will be given the supreme test. Can you determine what's missing and include it? Will you be able to take awkward sentence structure and transform it into glowing prose? Do you possess the courage, tact, and diplomacy to reject a submission or convince the author to rewrite it, tailoring it to meet your publication requirements? Editing can really run the gamut of writing and editing chores, and as you accept and resolve each new challenge, you'll have the satisfaction of knowing that you are building skills and techniques that will be useful to you no matter what the nature of your next writing assignment.

Newsletter Editing Tools

If you haven't had any relevant editing experience whatsoever, do a little background reading to acquaint yourself with the terminology and essential elements of editing. Locate some of the books on editing which we've listed in the bibliography and be prepared to refer to them often. Two specific titles that we've found most useful are *Editing Your Newsletter,* by Mark Beach and *The Newsletter*

Editor's Desk Book, by Marvin Arth and Helen Ashmore. Both are paperbacks and either or both would be good additions to your home library. They make great reference sources for the beginning editor, especially for such seemingly insignificant yet vital information as an analysis of copyediting procedures and the proper use of proofreaders' marks.

The toughest aspect of editing is reading for clarity and meaning and checking for accurate use of terminology. No matter how long you've edited, you will face new terminology that you'll need to verify. If you have a question about a term you can't resolve, you may ultimately need to consult with the author. The more thorough and accurate you are in your editing, the better your final product will look and read in print. Authors appreciate the careful editor who recognizes and corrects their casual blunders. It is painstaking, detailed work, but the results can be very rewarding, even if you are the only one who knows how much editorial work went into making the final product a success.

Before we leave this discussion of the tools of newsletter editing, we must mention word processors—both stand-alone and microcomputers using word processing software. Economics obviously will determine the amount and level of technology that can be used to produce the newsletter. If, however, your newsletter can afford the luxury of a microcomputer or dedicated word processor, your editing talents, combined with the economy of word processing, can make your editing efforts much more productive and the actual process of editing less time-consuming and far more cost-effective. If manuscripts are initially input into the word processor, the editing can be done directly from the keyboard with the resulting product ready for typesetting or printing. The formatting capabilities of the word processor allow pages to be arranged right justified with double or single columns, headers, footers, and other special enhancements that give the newsletter the image of a typeset, professional job.

Schedules and Deadlines

Nowhere is your ability to meet deadlines and schedule your work efficiently more important than with a newsletter. No matter what aspect of the newsletter you are associated with, you will constantly face deadlines and be required to produce according to schedules tailored to the expectations of printers, other editors, the publisher, and, of course, the subscriber. The more advance planning you are able to do and the more realistic the deadlines, the better your chances of survival. Unfortunately, not everyone in the publication chain will cooperate. Things can and will go wrong, and you may be called upon to perform some speedy and creative editorial maneuvers at the very last minute in order to produce an issue on schedule.

How you handle the occasional emergency will greatly affect your success as an editor. One such "emergency" that was experienced by one of the authors involved taking over an editing job for a small house organ published by a bank. It had been the practice of the former editor to receive all the articles, editorials, news clips, and assorted items via parcel post; they were all kept in a shoe box. The editor's job was to edit, assemble, and paste up the completed newsletter copy by the following week. Such an editing assignment was a big enough burden for the former editor, but when the new editor took over, without any advance preparation, no one to consult, and a week to put it all together, examples of editorial creativity and innovation surfaced that the new editor never dreamed of. The deadline was met and the bank never realized the magnitude of the editorial assignment. Your assignments probably won't approach that level of difficulty, but you'll have your opportunities to improvise to some degree, so be prepared.

Editing newsletters, especially the small ones, can be an exciting, enjoyable experience. The variety of assignments can be enormously rewarding. If you like challenges and tend to be self-reliant and innovative, you'll thrive as a newsletter editor.

EDITING PERIODICALS

The transition from editing newsletters to periodicals is a substantial one requiring an almost completely different approach. The newsletter is more demanding in terms of scheduling and deadlines and requires a considerable degree of flexibility and versatility on the part of the editor, who may be called upon to handle everything from layout to actual writing as well as editing.

Duties and Responsibilities

The periodical editor, more than the newsletter editor, tends to concentrate on identifying and corresponding with prospective authors and convincing them to submit articles for consideration. Even with those submissions that arrive unsolicited or "over the transom," the periodical editor must interact with the authors and review, evaluate, and consult everyone involved in the process of preparing manuscripts for publication. Actual editing of submissions is a significant part of a periodical editor's job. Because the articles received by the periodical are longer and more complex than newsletter submissions, the editor will have to be more knowledgeable about the subject matter and be able to tell at a glance what will be acceptable and what won't. If the editor isn't well-read and thoroughly grounded in the subject matter, the job of editing becomes onerous, the quality of the editing deteriorates, and ultimately, the overall quality of the publication suffers.

Soliciting Manuscripts

Assuming you've taken on editorial responsibilities for all or part of a periodical and that your periodical does not have a steady flow of unsolicited manuscript submissions, how do you ensure that there is enough material to meet publication deadlines?

- Use your own periodical to advertise your interest in submissions. If readers know you are seriously looking for authors, they may be motivated to contribute or at least express their interest through a query letter.
- Publish author guidelines in each issue along with an invitation for submissions.
- For special thematic issues planned in the future, search out potential authors whose subject interests are known to you, describe the particular issue you have in mind, and ask for a submission. Develop the habit of screening other periodicals to find authors who could make an effective contribution.
- When attending professional meetings, conferences, and workshops, make a point of introducing yourself to particularly successful speakers, and bring up the subject of writing an article. Take along a good supply of author guidelines, business cards, and even sample issues of your periodical and distribute them selectively. If you meet a potential author who seems interested in your publication, you've got something tangible to use to reinforce your discussion. Conferences and similar gatherings present excellent opportunities for locating potential authors.
- Follow up your new contacts with letters. Make certain you let the potential authors you've met under rather casual circumstances know that you are still interested in working with them.
- Contact the members of your advisory board frequently (if your periodical has one) and solicit their assistance in the search for potential authors. If your board constitutes a good cross section of the profession and if the members are truly serious about their supporting role, they can do wonders helping you locate authors from among their personal networks of colleagues and acquaintances.
- Develop a card file of names, addresses, and telephone numbers of authors, potential authors, and helpful contacts and revise and review it routinely. It will become a valuable asset as you develop your skills as a successful editor.

Managing Columns

Many periodicals use regular columns to keep their readers informed on subjects of current interest. The book review column, a column on microcomputers, or one on online database searching are all good examples. Readers who want to follow a particular subject will frequently turn first to their favorite column to see what's new. Including well-written columns in your periodical will not only produce more readers but can also spread the editorial responsibility, while, at the same time, providing a measure of editorial specialization. The column editor may choose to write much of the material appearing in the column and, even if using material contributed by others, will be responsible for editing it. Adding variety and interest to your periodical by using regular columns can be a real asset, but there are some potential pitfalls you'll need to recognize—pitfalls you'll encounter more often with columnists than with writers because you'll be working with them on a regular basis.

- Column editors have to meet the same or similar publication deadlines as all other writers.
- They may be several hundreds of miles away from you and be difficult to reach for consultation.
- They are subject to all of the many problems associated with life in the eighties and consequently may have to request deadline extensions or may—perish the thought—suddenly drop their column responsibilities altogether—and without notice.

How does the successful periodical editor avoid these pitfalls or cope with them if avoidance is impossible?

- Try to put your column editors on a schedule that will give you some leeway. Make sure their delivery deadlines are substantially earlier than your publication deadlines. That way you'll have a few weeks to make allowances for late arrivals or to substitute an article or another column if the columnist suddenly and without warning ceases to function altogether.
- Try to provide a backup author for your column who could take over on short notice. That's easier said than done, but if you plan for it and are on the lookout for just such a person, you'll be in a much better position to take appropriate steps when something does go wrong.

Remuneration

You may or may not receive a salary for what you do, and depending on the financial status of the periodical, you may or may not be able to offer financial rewards to your column editors and feature writers as an incentive. Such rewards can create a more positive attitude on the part of the column editor (as well as other regular contributors).

Special Features

Guest editorials, opinion pieces, and special features also help the editorial staff, even though they pose some special problems. If your publication uses editorials, you probably have the responsibility for coming up with the topics and doing the writing yourself. If you need an occasional break or could just use a fresh approach, offer the opportunity to submit a guest editorial to an author whose writing you admire and whose opinions tend to fit within the general scope of your publication. One or more guest editorials can produce enlightening opinions while, at the same time, giving you extra time to other editing tasks.

Opinion pieces written by people with something worth saying may result in considerable feedback from your readers—i.e., letters to the editor. Reader response is one of the few ways an editor can determine whether or not the publication is meeting its objectives. An especially controversial opinion piece can quickly move readers to respond with their own opinions. Good opinion pieces can lead to new columns and the inclusion of other material by the same author.

Special features often require special writers, especially when the topics become highly technical or require special expertise. It may be necessary to go outside the library profession and recruit writers from other fields to handle the subject matter adequately. Stress and burnout are currently "hot" topics, but the people who deal with them frequently and with credibility may come from other professions. It's often up to the editor to recognize these trends and seek out the best writers to do the job.

Picking a Title

If you happen to be involved at the inception of the periodical and have an opportunity to engage in the prepublication planning and design work, you may be given a chance to influence the selection of a title. That's a fairly significant moment in the life of a periodical. Some publishers change the names of their periodicals fairly frequently. If you listen to serials librarians, you'll think that the names change with amazing frequency. Settling on a title that you can live with indefinitely is no simple task, but it has to be done. As you go through the title selection process, ask yourself these questions:

- Is the title unique? Has it ever been used before?
- Will it receive universal acceptance? Does it mean the same thing to the majority of potential readers?
- Is it easy to remember? Should it be shortened or abbreviated to make it more manageable?
- Will it stand the test of time and still be just as meaningful 20 years from now?
- Does it fit the scope of the publication or will it imply limitations that you may find difficult to live with in the future?

Working with Specialists

There are people with special talents whom you will need to assist you in your publication endeavors. They have skills and training that fall outside your areas of expertise. As you prepare to work with them, analyze the best approach to take in order to have an effective working relationship with them. Learn their rules and jargon and what can reasonably be expected and in what time frame. Lead time is necessary in many artistic and printing processes. Reimbursement for materials and services is expected, so you'll have to build these expenses into your budget.

Artists

Most artists expect to be paid for their labors. They set rates according to the job, on a per piece basis or at an agreed-to hourly rate. Before you begin working with an artist, make certain that you have a written agreement specifying such things as:

- The cost of various types of finished artwork and conditions under which prices will be allowed to change.
- The condition or quality of the finished work—what you'll accept and what you won't.
- Delivery dates.
- Who holds copyright to the artwork submitted for publication.
- Any limitations or restrictions on quantity requested. Some artists are unable to produce in quantity.
- Conditions under which either party can terminate the agreement and how they would go about doing so.
- The period of time to be covered and conditions for renewal.

If you are making arrangements for a reasonably long-term association with an artist, the more care and thought you put into your operating agreement, the better your association will be and the easier it will be to resolve any differences that might surface.

Photographers

Photographers fall under roughly the same classification as artists, and in your relationship to them, the same general rules apply. You'll probably be dealing with more than one photographer and some will be amateurs while others will be professionals.

Photographers as well as artists appreciate receiving credit for their work whether or not they are paid for their efforts. So don't forget to include an appropriate credit line for every photograph published, either under the photograph itself or at least in a list of photo credits printed somewhere in the publication.

Quality is the watchword when it comes to selecting photographs. It is usually preferable to refrain from using a photograph altogether if the quality of the one submitted does not measure up to your standards. What you want are high-contrast, well-defined, quality black-and-white photographs that will reproduce well. If in doubt, consult your printer, who will be able to give you detailed specifications. If you find yourself using photographs on a regular basis, you should plan to build your requirements into your author guidelines.

Printers

Another specialist you may work with is the printer. Depending on the particular publication, you may be required to take the production process all the way through to the final product as it emerges from the print shop. If you have to deal with the printer, take some time to do a little basic research on printing before you disgrace yourself by asking for the impossible.

- Learn the terminology printers use so you'll both be speaking the same language.
- Find out what your printer can and cannot do so that you won't be asking for the impossible.
- Observe the printer's deadlines.
- If your printer is located nearby, try to arrange for a personal tour of the print shop. Use that tour to begin to build a good working relationship. The potential for success increases dramatically when printer and editor both strive for maximum cooperation and understanding.

Marketing Staff

Somewhere in the editorial process, you may be called upon to work with the marketing and promotion staff of your publication. They handle subscriptions, promote your product by advertising in other publications, and arrange for the sale of space to organizations interested in advertising in your publication. You can contribute to effective marketing of your publication by keeping future sales in the back of your mind as you work with authors and design issues. Lively, thought-provoking and stimulating articles, columns, and editorials will result in a quality periodical. If you've done all you can to make the periodical an attractive publication, your marketing and promotion colleagues will have a much easier job promoting your product.

EDITING SKILLS

You are not going to undertake an editorial assignment without having had some background in writing and editing. If you are concerned about your editorial shortcomings, you can certainly consult a number of helpful books on the subject. Your best source of support and assistance, however, is professional literature. Steep yourself in the professional literature regularly and religiously to find out:

- What current topics are of interest to librarians.
- Who the major contributors to the literature and trend-setters in the profession are.
- Which topics are just beginning to attract interest.
- Which topics have begun to fade or have already been written about.

We live in a trendy society and our professional interests tend to follow similar peaks and valleys. In the late 1960s and early 1970s, academic librarianship was involved with approval plans. That interest was reflected in a series of conferences, workshops, books, and articles, all treating the subject in detail. The approval plan is no longer a trendy topic and has given way to such subjects as the use of microcomputers in libraries and collection management. The successful periodical editor will recognize these trends as they emerge and locate the articles and authors early in order to keep the periodical in the forefront of professional interests and activities. The more reading you do, the more conferences and professional meetings you attend, and the more attention you give to developing and maintaining your personal network of authors and other contacts, the more successful you'll become as an editor.

Writing for Presentation

From time to time, you may be asked to speak at a conference or seminar, or you may be asked to be a panelist or respond to a call for contributed papers. Before you instantly agree to do so, consider that writing a presentation for a conference or seminar, no matter how large or small the audience, is not easy. The presentation must be appropriate to the theme of the meeting, must be more entertaining than a published paper, and must fit within a certain time limit. Even meeting these criteria does not guarantee a successful presentation. The degree to which it will be effective depends to a great extent on the appearance, personality, and charm of the presenter and his/her ability to relate to the topic and the audience.

PREPARATION

If, on the one hand, you are asked to make a presentation at a conference, you will probably be given an assigned topic and little latitude in which to vary your presentation. If, on the other hand, you are responding to a call for papers, you will have the option of determining your topic within the general framework of the conference theme, based on your own knowledge and experience. Your aim here is to select a topic which is of interest to the potential audience.

Any paper presented at a meeting, whether the keynote speech or a contributed paper, is going to take a great deal of research to produce. If you are the keynote speaker, you may be presenting ideas that are designed to generate interest or create an atmosphere around which the conference can then take place. Your speech may be a summary of the connecting ideas for the meeting—the very reason the meeting is being held. If you are the keynote speaker, you were selected on the basis of your reputation, your knowledge, your visibility, your connection with the theme, or a combination of all these. If you are making the keynote speech or one of the major presentations, your ideas—rather than facts and statistics—may become the focus of the speech and less formal research will be necessary. You will then have a greater opportunity for creativity within the context of a major presentation.

If you are submitting a contributed paper, you will probably be asked to submit your idea, then write an abstract, and, finally, present a draft of the paper. A group of referees will read the submitted papers and then decide which ones will be accepted for actual presentation. Only then, after having done all this work, will you know for sure that your paper has been accepted. Once it is accepted, you will have the opportunity to polish the writing; you may also have to submit a camera-ready copy to the conference organizers so that the paper will be available for the participants or will be ready for publication as part of the formal conference proceedings.

If you are preparing a contributed paper, you are probably speaking on a very narrow topic about which you have a great deal of knowledge and experience. However, even in this situation, you will still be doing a certain amount of research to present opposing ideas and alternative methodologies. If by chance the conference is cancelled, or your paper is not accepted for presentation, don't simply toss it in the trash. Take some time to review it. Do any rewriting necessary and then submit it to another conference for presentation or rewrite it for publication. Even if your paper is accepted for presentation, if you find out after the conference is over that the paper will not be published as part of the proceedings, don't let that research go to waste. Rewrite the paper, removing the elements that made it suitable for presentation, and then submit it for publication to a relevant periodical.

Whatever the circumstances under which you are presenting the paper, at some point you must begin writing. There are several basic steps to follow, similar to those used when writing for publication.

RESEARCH

Jot down the ideas around which you plan to write your presentation. Conduct a manual or online literature search and be prepared to include not only library publications but also literature in other fields related to your topic. Consider carefully the theme of the conference. What do you have to say that is relevant? Consider your chosen topic. How can you make it relate to the theme?

Doing research for an oral presentation is similar to the research you would do for an article or a book. However, you should be more alert for incidents, anecdotes, particular information that will lend itself to an oral presentation. Columns of figures may go a long way toward supporting your thesis, but they will be difficult if not impossible for you to present and for your listeners to follow, even with visual aids such as slides and transparencies. Instead, find a way to summarize them. The audience you confuse, you will lose.

Look for attention-grabbing data or personal situations you can relate that will make your audience stay through the last word of your presentation. It's important to stress the human qualities. Friendly, even folksy presentations have a way of attracting attention because they reveal a real person behind the lectern, not a robotic mannequin.

WRITING

Before writing, prepare an outline. This need not be a formal English-class-perfect outline, but it does need to be functional. It may simply be nothing more than a listing of ideas around which you wish to frame your paper. After you have put together this outline, play with it, reorganizing it to provide the most effective presentation of your ideas. Keep in mind that you are writing for an audience who will be listening to, not reading, your words. You must attract and hold their attention. To do so, your ideas must be presented clearly and concisely. Because your audience cannot reread your ideas, they must absorb them upon hearing them. Keep the attention span of your audience in mind as you put together the ideas and concepts you want to present. If you end up making your presentation too technical or complex, you risk losing your audience as well as earning a reputation as a poor presenter.

Present your ideas, starting slowly, perhaps with an anecdote, humorous or otherwise, and then build to one or more main points. At the end of the presentation, summarize your ideas, perhaps by listing specifically what you want the audience to retain. Unless they are feverishly taking notes, it will be important for you to make it easy for them to take home the essence of what you had to say.

Use conversational English, not the more formal English you might use if you were writing a paper for publication. Stiff, formal language will not only detract from the message you want to get across, it will lose the attention of your audience.

As you prepare your outline, and later, as you write the paper, think in terms of possible audiovisual aids you might use. Such aids will be particularly important if you are doing comparisons, using statistics, or listing a series of steps or phases. Also, if you cite important definitions, you can use overhead transparencies with the definitions on them so the audience can write them down. Or you can make copies of them and use them as handouts for your audience. Visuals, if properly prepared, make your presentation easier for your listeners to follow, and they will not have to take as many notes if you provide them with actual handouts created from these visuals. Computer-produced charts, graphs, and spreadsheets are all transferable to overhead transparencies so you needn't redo them once you have them put together.

If you decide to prepare computer-generated visuals, attempt to have them produced on a plotter with color capability. The results will be outstanding and your audience will appreciate the difference.

As you design your audiovisual aids, keep in mind that, depending on your topic, they can be your greatest help in relating your ideas. They can also be your greatest disaster if they are poorly prepared or if you do not use the equipment effectively. If you are not an audiovisual expert, seek professional advice from your library staff, the campus audiovisual center personnel, or a store specializing in audiovisual equipment. Seek out media experts and ask for assistance. Audiovisual presentations must be well-designed to be effective. Don't expect your audience to read many lines of type or to follow an overly elaborate or intricate workflow chart. Make the aids as simple and as clear as possible and always try them out on staff or colleagues before you add them to your presentation. When you view your visual creations, sit in the back of the room. If you have trouble deciphering what is up on the screen, be prepared to return to the drawing board and fix your mistakes. Some sources of information that will help you prepare for an oral presentation are listed at the end of this chapter.

In designing your visual aids and making your presentation, plan to stand in such a way that you will face your audience, not the screen. Your voice will project better and you will be able to gauge the audience reaction to your visuals. If your back is toward your audience, you'll never know if they are delighted or confused by what you have projected on the screen.

If at all possible, provide handouts for your audience. These could include reproductions of your visuals, a bibliography, or even a brief outline of your presentation. Not only will the audience be able to refer to these handouts afterward, but they can also use them to jot down notes that pertain to specific items listed on the handouts. However, a handout can be as potentially disastrous as those audio or visual aids if it is not of good quality, well-produced, relevant to the presentation, and readable.

In the preceding paragraphs, we've referred to "audio" materials as well as visuals. Depending on the nature of your presentation, it is entirely possible that you will need to provide your audience with excerpts from audiotapes or some other audio source. It is important that the audience be able to hear it clearly, so use the same care and planning in the design of the audio material as you would use with your visuals. Make certain that the sound equipment you use is of a high enough quality so that the sound can be heard by everyone in the audience. If you are making the presentation at some remote location, be prepared to give the conference planners the specifications for the technical equipment you'll need to make your audio and visual presentations work smoothly. If you can't carry the technical support with you, it will be up to you to work out the arrangements for what you need with others. You can't begin that process too soon.

PANEL PRESENTATIONS

If you are asked to be a panelist at a conference, there are several things you should consider. Be sure at the outset that you will have either access to the main speakers' presentations before the discussion so that you can prepare your reaction in advance or at least have an outline of what the speaker will be saying. If you are the reactor, it will be essential that you be prepared to listen carefully and make notes during the course of the presentation. If there are questions from the audience, be sure to make notes of the questions and the answers so you can refer to them, citing points accurately if called up to do so.

One kind of panel presentation has the main speaker presenting a point of view and the other panelists reacting. Another kind has each member of the panel making a presentation about a part or variation of a general idea or topic. Yet another type of panel involves the audience by allowing them to ask the panelists questions based on their reactions to a general topic. Before you agree to be a panel member, be sure that you know exactly what kind of panel is being planned so that you will be fully prepared and ready for your particular role.

REHEARSALS

Before you make your actual presentation, set up a few practice sessions and at least one dress rehearsal. The practice sessions can take several forms: reading your presentation aloud, perhaps facing a mirror; or reading it into a tape recorder and playing it back for a little self-evaluation. Practicing in front of a mirror allows you to see your "body language" and become conscious of any particular quirks you didn't know you had. Either method allows you to clock your presentation to be sure you fit the allocated time period. The dress rehearsal should be before a friend or colleague who is willing to make an honest critique of your presentation. You should allow 1¼ to 1½ minutes of reading time per page (typed and double-spaced). This allows you to breathe properly, lets your audience take brief notes, and sets a pace that is not too fast for the audience to follow. If you use an overhead projector, you may find yourself speaking even more slowly as you deliberately slow down to handle the transparencies.

Recording your presentation will give you an opportunity to listen to your speech patterns, detect any hints of nervousness, and assess your attitude toward the audience. Don't speak too quickly. Don't sound condescending. Don't sound too dogmatic. Strive for a smooth delivery, evenly paced and carefully articulated.

If possible, practice the presentation before a larger group. If your organization encourages employees to participate in outside activities and to make formal presentations, you may have an opportunity to practice on your peers. Some libraries have a regularly scheduled time for staff to practice presenting their ideas, their papers, or their research to their colleagues. There are at least three advantages to this arrangement:

1. The presenter has the opportunity to get feedback from colleagues;

2. The presenter has the opportunity to become familiar with presenting the paper or speech; and

3. Colleagues have the chance to hear a presentation that they might miss otherwise.

If such sessions are going to succeed, both the presenter and the audience must realize that this is an opportunity to provide frank appraisals of the presentiation so that the speaker has the option of revising the paper, improving the presentation, or correcting problems with the material.

Don't be afraid to ask for assistance. If a colleague is a particularly effective speaker, ask him/her to give you some pointers after listening to your presentation. Consider joining a local group that makes speeches and critiques them. Investigate the possibility of taking a continuing education course designed to help you make successful public presentations.

On the day of your presentation, don't walk into the room cold and expect everything to be ready for you. Check out the room, the acoustics, the microphone, and the placement of the lectern in advance. You may find that you need a reading light if the general room lighting is very dim or if you are using audiovisual aids. Learn how to adjust the microphone. Practice with the microphone to be sure you know when it is on, how close you must be to it, and how your voice projects. Of course, all this must be done in advance, before the sessions begin. It means getting there early, but it will be worth the time you spend.

FORUMS

How do you decide where you are going to present a paper? There are different forums such as local or regional organizational meetings, as well as national conferences. There are subject-oriented programs, both within and without the library field. Such forums may give you an opportunity to present library-related papers to an entirely new audience, or they may give you a chance to present your research on a topic not confined to the library field. Examples include making presentations on bibliographic instruction to the Modern Language Association or giving a paper on quality circles in higher education to a regional education association.

There are theme conferences on automation or collection development, and if you have expertise in these areas, they can be natural forums for you. There are divisional conferences, such as ACRL or LITA, as well as numerous other opportunities to present your ideas. Be discriminating and attempt to pick the ones that most closely fit your interests.

Locally, you can create visibility for your library and, at the same time, practice your presentations by speaking to service clubs. Don't overlook the opportunity to develop your own expertise in making those presentations to colleagues. You might even start by putting together a workshop for staff on communication, dealing with problem patrons, or database searching.

TRAINING WORKSHOPS AND SEMINARS

Training workshops and seminars are the one- or two-person traveling shows that are increasing in popularity as librarians become more involved in nontraditional activities that require some kind of specialized training or at least familiarization beyond what's offered in the basic instruction manual. Take the microcomputer for instance.

How many brochures advertising microcomputer workshops have come across your desk in the last couple of years? You might think that after the first two or three in your area, everyone who needed training or background in the new technology would have gotten it. But the brochures keep coming and the microcomputer training workshops continue as one of the all-time best drawing cards on the workshop circuit. Other popular workshops include how to write successful grant proposals, private and public, and how to get the most out of your OCLC M300 (a workshop that has taken off already in those areas where networks perform only minimally when it comes to providing training).

What do these workshops provide that keeps the audiences interested? A combination of hand-holding, motivation, confidence building, and a sense of security. Who are the successful training workshop leaders? People who obviously know their material, but also people who have developed and perfected the knack of making effective presentations. In many cases, what they have to say is less important than how they say it. They have learned to build enthusiasm, motivate, and offer encouragement to the extent that the workshop attendee can go home with a collection of new ideas, concepts, and techniques, certainly, but most of all with a new sense of confidence and a feeling of enthusiasm about something that was avoided previously. The successful grant proposal writing workshop is the one that motivates a participant to sit down and write a winning proposal. It happens—and fairly frequently. All the successful proposal writer really needed was a burst of enthusiasm brought about by a dynamic workshop leader with a "can do" attitude and a list of fail-safe tips and suggestions. The dynamic microcomputer workshop leader can motivate the almost-decided PC purchaser right into the nearest computer store. The same thing goes for the OCLC M300 users who are exposed to a similar session in user motivation.

So where do you come in? Conducting a workshop is nothing like presenting a paper at a conference or serving on a reactor panel—or is it? What is the writing connection? You come in if you have some expertise to share with your colleagues. If you have a specialty, whether it is proposal writing, disaster planning, preservation, or microcomputer training, you can share it with others. But once you've identified your specialty, you've got to make an honest appraisal of your ability to put together the whole workshop package from beginning to end and be able to handle the role of motivator consistently and convincingly for perhaps a daylong session. To conduct a workshop successfully takes all of the many skills we've described and more. Here are some of the workshop duties and responsibilities you'll need to be able to master:

- Prepare a presentation that will cover the topic in detail and serve as an effective learning module.

- Design and prepare pertinent and attention-getting handouts and audiovisual materials that will supplement your presentation.
- Incorporate motivational techniques and devices that will not only keep your audience interested but enthusiastic.
- Provide ideas, concepts, tips, and suggestions that can be taken back to the workplace and applied to real situations.
- Handle all of the business aspects of putting on the show. That may include advertising, handling payments (if you are going to charge a fee), transportation, and other logistical considerations.

An intimidating prospect? It certainly is, but for those willing and talented enough to carry it off, the potential rewards are enormously enticing. Here are a few to consider:

- The successful workshop planner/designer/leader has almost unlimited possibilities for turning workshop material directly into articles, books, and a variety of other writing projects.
- Your success with your microcomputer workshops will without doubt lead you to other opportunities. The successful workshop series gives you a track record that will encourage others to seek you out to undertake a variety of projects.
- The contacts you make will prove valuable to your career and will enhance your networking capability.
- The work you generate in the name of dynamic leadership—selling your ideas—motivating others—will certainly add to your net worth as a confident leader whatever your status in the library hierarchy.
- Best of all, you will have the personal satisfaction of having received recognition of your talents as a writer and as a presenter. When you've achieved the status of a successful workshop leader, you'll find yourself in the enviable position of being able to entertain the idea of more writing and speaking opportunities than you can handle.

Aim for the broadest audience for your ideas as possible. And don't forget the international conferences. They are often held within reasonable flying distance of your home base, and if you can afford the expense, they open up lots of possibilities for widening your list of contacts and presentations.

All of these opportunities, if pursued, will make you a better and more relaxed speaker. You will experience anxiety the first few times you present. But as you become more relaxed, you will find these anxieties disappearing though they may never disappear completely. Even show business veterans insist they still have occasional bouts of nervousness before appearances.

Any time you make a presentation, you not only provide visibility for yourself but also for your library and your ideas. And making a presentation adds another entry for your resumé and increases your network of contacts. Almost any presentation has the potential to be turned into an article, a chapter, or even a book proposal. A paper written for a conference may become a part of the published conference proceedings, but while awaiting publication, may reach a larger audience through publication in a national periodical. Naturally, each time the same material is used, some revising and modifying will be necessary. This particular book, for example, was conceived as a result of a series of presentations about writing and publishing.

Every time you take the time and energy to research a topic, try to squeeze every bit of value from the material you acquire. With a little ingenuity and some thoughtful planning, you'll be surprised at what you can accomplish.

SELECTED SOURCES

Challis, A. James, and Alley, Brian. "Can You Hear Me at the Back of the Room?" *Technicalities* 2 (July 1982): 12–15.

Green, Lee. *101 Ways to Use the Overhead Projector.* Littleton, CO: Libraries Unlimited, 1982.

Koslov, Marcia J. "Competency, Conduct and Conference: How to Be Effective at Meetings." In *Women and Library Management: Theories, Skills and Values,* edited by Darlene E. Weingand, pp. 55–70. Ann Arbor, MI: Pierian Press, 1982.

Lord, Robert. *Running Conventions, Conferences, and Meetings.* New York: Amacon, 1981.

HOTEL

Establishing Your Reputation

Now that you've had some successful experiences editing, writing, and making presentations, the more people who know about your talents, the better. If the editors and publishers who are looking for material don't know you exist, they aren't going to think of your name the next time they are looking for someone to handle a particular writing project. Editors in search of writing talent will often maintain a collection of names of those writers who are specialists of one kind or another and who are well-known among their colleagues as authorities, recognized experts, or at least popular proponents of a particular philosophy. Each has a reputation which has been built, consciously or otherwise over a period of time, by writing primarily along the lines of some particular area of specialization. Armed with a list of known talent, an editor can usually line up a willing writer to handle an assignment. Such a list is invaluable both to the editor searching for an author and the author whose reputation has earned him/her a spot on one or more editor/publisher lists.

Such writers are easily recognizable for specific areas of concentration because they have made a reputation by focusing on particular areas and then writing extensively. The more they have written—or spoken on a subject—the more they have been asked to write, to chair or serve on committees, organize and present workshops, provide consulting services, or serve as conference keynote speakers. For many of them, managing their writing projects and speaking engagements has become a major concern. As their popularity has increased, so have the demands on their time. That's not a problem for you at the moment, but as you become more active and more visible in the profession, you will find that it will become increasingly necessary to decide which projects to accept and which to reject. Determining which ones will provide you with the greatest rewards in terms of your career goals may be a pleasant experience to anticipate.

GETTING STARTED

Assuming that you agree with the premise that visibility in the profession is an important factor in establishing a reputation, what are some specific things you can consider doing in order to become more visible?

- Attend professional meetings which deal with your areas of interest.
- Volunteer for committee assignments.
- Write letters to editors commenting on articles of particular interest to you.
- Keep up to date by reading professional literature.
- Make a concerted effort to establish personal contacts at professional meetings with people with like interests.
- Make presentations at conferences.
- Lead or participate in seminars and workshops.
- Get cited in the literature whenever and wherever possible.

Building your reputation isn't something in which you engage every time you happen to think of it. It is a constant activity that can become part of a general plan. If you take the time to consider reputation building and the variety of things you can do to enhance your own image, you can set goals that will lead toward establishing and enhancing your reputation and then during a specific time period, work toward accomplishing them. What are some goals you think you can accomplish this year that will assist you as you attempt to make a name for yourself? Make a list. Take the ones you think you can accomplish and put a realistic completion date opposite each. Next, note the goals on your desk calendar at work where they will serve as reminders. At the end of the period you've allotted, take stock. Review your accomplishments, add new goals, and revise and reevaluate the ones you failed to achieve.

Once again, it takes resolve, determination, and consistent follow-through to achieve goals of any type. If self-image and reputation are important areas where you need to improve, you can do so with some planning and lots of determination. The benefits in terms of recognition, contacts, new projects, and assignments are truly significant for the writer, speaker, and career professional.

PROFESSIONAL MEETINGS

Do you know how much it costs to attend a major conference these days? An arm and a leg is an old expression that offers an appropriate answer in lieu of supplying a detailed financial breakdown. It is a substantial expenditure, and yet to several thousand information science professionals who attend SLA, ALA (both the Annual Conferences and the Midwinter Meetings), ASIS, and the regionals, it is a legitimate expenditure. No, they don't all receive full funding from their respective organizations. Far from it. Most of the conference goers pay a large part, if not all, of their expenses themselves. Each one has different reasons for attending, ranging from altruistic professionalism to just wanting to get away from Podunk for a few days. Somewhere in between are the people who see the professional meeting as an opportunity to wheel and deal, if you will, with like-minded colleagues. It is a three- or four-day opportunity to get to know people, make contacts, do a little networking, consult, connive, and conspire. And if you plan your conference and budget your time in accordance with your predetermined conference goals, you are bound to come away with a sense of accomplishment and the belief that it was worth the effort and expense. You did make some good contacts. You accomplished a satisfactory portion of your objectives. You now know more people and more people know you. You have become more visible in the profession and your participation in your professional organization has become a more productive investment for your membership fees and travel dollars.

How do you make certain that attendance at a meeting will pay off for you? Plan ahead and begin by making a list of exactly what it is you want to accomplish while there. Draw up an itinerary and start filling in the blanks with meetings, appointments, and events you don't want to miss. The itinerary doesn't have to be anything elaborate, just a written plan that you will use to keep you on the track meeting your commitments and using your time wisely. How are you going to have any fun tied to a detailed conference timetable? Build in all the fun you require right there on your itinerary. You are your own conference planner, so how you allocate your time is entirely up to you. Just remember, your total time is limited, so as inviting as the impromptu shopping trips to Marshall Field's or Neiman-Marcus may be, they are going to reduce your available time for making contacts and getting to know and be known in the profession.

Don't forget to plan visits to libraries in the conference area if you have a particular interest that makes such a visit potentially valuable. But be sure to make arrangements in advance. Nobody appreciates the unannounced visitor. Most visits are easy to set up with a phone call or letter. Once you've made the appointment, be certain to confirm it with a follow-up note to the host. Making the best impression possible before you arrive will help ensure a good reputation. Your careful advance planning will mark you as a serious visitor.

Preparing the itinerary at home when you can devote the time to it is far better than deciding on the fly, when the conference is already in session. Last-minute planning leads to confusion, missed appointments and meetings, and a considerable letdown for you when you review the missed opportunities at the end of the conference. The careful, advance planner will call ahead and work out meeting times and dates with people who are important to see. They will then know that you are serious and that you consider the appointment important, and as a consequence, they will make every effort to accommodate you. Trying to set up a meeting at the last minute when you are actually on the scene at a busy conference rarely produces acceptable results. Not only that, but the person you want to contact could be inconvenienced by your last-minute request, thus reducing the value of any meeting that results. If you didn't make plans, the other person probably did and simply won't be able to meet with you at all. However, if you are organized, you will have no trouble determining how to respond to someone who wants to set up a meeting with you at the last minute. A quick look at your itinerary will tell you where, when, and if you have the time to spare.

With your well-organized itinerary in hand, you are ready to proceed. As you attend meetings, work with committees, and make contacts at parties and social events, deliberately seek out people you would like to meet and introduce yourself. The person you want to meet may already have become well-known. You are on the way. If you don't take the initiative, you probably won't get introduced. As you build your confidence and widen your circle of acquaintances, you'll be surprised, if you didn't already guess, that you are beginning to build a list of names to which you've mentally tied topics of interest. Before you forget the names, start making a collection of them in the form of business cards, those handy little sources of information that provide the names and addresses that make it easy for you to renew contacts after the conference ends. You don't have any of your own? If your organization won't supply them, there's nothing to prevent you from having your own printed and exchanging them with colleagues. Collect cards from people you especially don't want to lose track of and, when you get home, be prepared to transfer the information to your card file or other name/address file or file them alphabetically in specially designed business card folders commonly available in stationery stores. Microcomputer users can use specially designed software to store name and address files on disks.

If you've designed your itinerary carefully, you will have left plenty of blank space to accommodate any last-minute changes. Meetings have a habit of being cancelled, meeting room numbers change, and you'll want space to write in the changes. Handy telephone numbers to note on your itinerary include those for your hotel as well as other conference hotels, your airline, and restaurants where you have reservations. You can locate most of those numbers before you leave home. Having them on your itinerary will save you lots of time at the conference.

All this talk about careful, detailed conference planning with itineraries organized in advance may sound like so much needless regimentation. If it does, just try to remember what you spent at your last major conference. Did your investment of several hundred dollars pay off for you? Can you honestly say that you couldn't have profited from some care and attention to planning? If you think about it for very long, chances are you'll agree that more advance planning could have made your conference investment more of a success. Yes, it all takes time: making the conference itinerary, plugging in the appointments and meetings, but once you've tried it, we know you'll agree that it was a worthwhile investment of your time.

VOLUNTEER COMMITTEE ASSIGNMENTS

One guaranteed way to break into an organization is to volunteer for committee assignments. It is a great way to meet the people who can be categorized as the "doers" of the profession and an even better way to find out how the organization works and its goals and objectives. "Know Your Audience" is a familiar dictum of the successful public speaker. Here, it might well be modified to "Know Your Organization." As a member of committees, you are one of the best-placed people when it comes to gaining an understanding of just how the organization works. For a writer, the committee assignment can be a gold mine of topics, ideas, and inspiration. What better vantage point is there if you intend to write about what's happening in the profession? If you need expert opinions, advice, and general guidance, the movers and shakers who can provide it are the committee members. Committees are always looking for volunteers, major professional organizations use their professional journals to advertise for volunteers at least once a year. One caveat should be noted here: Many committee assignments involve lots of hours of hard work so don't volunteer unless you are seriously ready and willing to contribute your fair share. Committee assignments usually require your involvement at various times throughout the year, not only at conferences.

LETTERS TO THE EDITOR

Writing letters to the editor as a means of building your professional reputation is not as corny as it sounds. Of course, any dolt can write a letter to an editor. Thousands do it every day. What we're suggesting is a bit more reasonable and responsible and, we hope, productive. As you read the literature and react to various articles, use the letter to the editor to raise objections, praise the author, or suggest alternatives. Editors depend on a certain number of such letters in their mailboxes, but the ones they like to publish are those with substance. If you have a sensible point to make, do it. Not only is it important to speak out on issues of substance, it is equally important to share your opinions with your colleagues. Your reputation may be enhanced by the quality of your letter, so you'll want to review it critically before you send it off. For the sender, the letter means visibility, the potential for more contacts, and, depending on the relative merit of its contents, possibly an invitation to write something for publication.

Whenever you have a genuinely positive reaction to an author's work and want to express your comments, write a letter. Authors like to know that their works are read, and they take a certain amount of pleasure in receiving comments from their readers. When you generate such a letter, it is yet another way to make contacts.

SELECTING YOUR PROFESSIONAL READING

A successful writer in the information science profession needs to keep up on the professional literature. You have to know what's being written about and who is doing the writing. If you have narrowed your field of interests down to a specific set of topics or subject areas, it is more important than ever to know all you can about those areas of interest and about the writing competition. You can't get that kind of information by reading selectively. You've got to organize your reading habits into a formal, routine system that will assure you that you are always aware of what's current in your area. There may be a dozen or so journals that regularly cover your interests. A quick scanning of the table of contents of each issue may provide sufficient notice to alert you to any specific articles you want to read. Religiously scanning the 12 issues each month will give you all of the information you need to fuel your personal idea factory for future articles and writing projects. You'll be able to spot trends as stock market analysts do, and as a writer, you'll have exactly the kind of clues you need to predict what is needed. With that information in hand, you can time or plan your writing projects accordingly. Regular reading of the literature is a must.

GETTING CITED IN THE LITERATURE

This is a topic that needs to be discussed, yet it is one that we know in advance will be received with a variety of reactions, both positive and negative. It is our belief that citations are important to writers. They constitute a means of establishing a name in the field, and the sheer numbers of citations for a given work provide an indication of the degree or level of interest on the part of scholars, researchers, and other writers. In academic circles, counting citations has been proposed as one way of establishing criteria for professors standing for tenure. The reasoning here is based on the belief that if Professor X is widely cited in the literature, those citations indicate his/her standing as a recognized scholar in the field.

One of the great proponents of citation counting is Eugene Garfield, president and founder of the Institute for Scientific Information. He is a firm believer in the value of analyzing citation statistics, and his various citation indexes are well-received and widely used not only in the bibliographic searching process but also by the bean counters who are interested in finding out something more about individual writers and researchers and the relative popularity of their articles. (For more on the subject, read Garfield's "Citations and Games Scientists Play, or, The Citation Index Game," *Current Contents,* 31: July 31, 1974 [reprinted in *Essays of an Information Scientist,* by Eugene Garfield, published by ISI Press in 1977].)

Our interest in being cited in the literature relates directly to building a reputation as a recognized writer in a professional field. As you write, you will no doubt cite other authors. If your writing is significant and worthy of being cited in the work of another, your name will appear in footnotes and bibliographies. The more you write, the greater the number of citations accruing to your name. Being cited frequently in the literature may not result in a favorable tenure decision from your colleagues at Old Siwash U, but it will definitely provide you with recognition as a regular and established contributor to the literature. That achievement will, in turn, open up other possibilities in terms of your career and your professional and job contacts as well as more possibilities for advancing your writing activities.

NETWORKING

The feminist press has had a lot to say about the value of networking in succeeding on the job. The principles advocated regularly in the pages of *Ms., Working Woman,* and *Savvy* for women who want to get ahead in the business world have numerous applications for writers (male and female) breaking into professional writing. Making contacts is the name of the game and maintaining and developing those contacts is part of the skill that you will need to acquire in order to make networking pay off for you.

Whatever your particular writing interests may be, having a large number of acquaintances is bound to help you as you search for information related to your writing projects. For example, a committee assignment for a national professional association puts you in touch with a number of like-minded colleagues. You meet with them a couple of times a year and probably correspond with them frequently in between meetings. In the course of that committee assignment, you will, if you make the effort, get to know certain individuals with whom you may have interests in common. Out of these new friendships can come a variety of benefits that may directly affect your writing. Contacts produce more contacts, and before you know it, you have the names and addresses of a number of people whose background and interests you know and who, at some point in the future, you may call upon for assistance. We should point out here that the object in networking is not entirely self-serving. It is a two-way process involving you as the potential provider of assistance as well. This mutual sharing concept, if carried to its logical conclusion, will benefit all of the networkers. It's part of the reason that people of like interest anywhere find it easier to succeed in the world if they have a wide range of friendships and acquaintances. Becoming part of some kind of an active network is a must for anyone who hopes to achieve success as a writer in the information science field.

To be an effective networker, you've got to keep in mind points that will help you become a trusted, reliable member of such an informal support group.

- When you are asked to assist with a conference, workshop, presentation, or other similar gathering, make a concerted effort to carry out your responsibilities cheerfully and thoroughly.
- Be prompt. Meet deadlines.
- When colleagues shirk responsibilities and you can lend additional assistance, don't hesitate.
- Be alert for new contacts and information that will lead to other assignments or projects in which you might like to become involved.
- Thank your conference contact formally for having been given the opportunity to be involved.

THE IMPORTANCE OF POLITICS

We are all political animals to some degree and never was a healthy regard for politics more important than it is for writers. Tact, diplomacy, and a sense of politics can spell the difference between getting permission for an interview and losing out altogether. As you approach colleagues, publishers, editors, and other writers in the course of carrying out your writing projects, establishing your reputation for dependability, trust, and maintaining confidences will pay substantial dividends as you build your publications list. People in the writing and publishing business tend to be serious, sensitive, and hard-working. They will expect the same degree of commitment from you.

REPUTATIONS: GOOD AND BAD

Establishing and enhancing your reputation is something you never stop doing. Hopefully, your efforts will be directed toward building the kind of reputation that will allow you to practice your writing skills whenever and wherever you please. You will have the contacts and will be well-established in terms of professional support groups, networks, and associations and committee memberships. Your name, while not exactly a household word, will be widely known as a capable writer of substance. There are those with bad reputations, of course. Ask any editor or conference planner and you'll get a complete rundown of the primary characteristics. It's easy to earn such a reputation. All you have to do is miss deadlines consistently, miss appointments, drop the ball on assignments, fail to deliver on promises, and commit other equally unappealing blunders. Once you are tagged with such a reputation, it will be difficult to lose it. That's why keeping your reputation uppermost in your mind as you establish yourself as a talented, capable career professional is essential in your writing program.

CONCLUSION

In the preceding chapters, we've attempted to provide you with a variety of avenues from which to approach writing in the literature of your profession. We have suggested ways to get started and to grow as your skills develop. Although this book is intended to address the process of getting published, we have also taken the liberty of including ideas and suggestions involving networking and becoming involved in professional organizations, as well as a host of other activities, all of which have a connection with writing and publishing your thoughts and ideas. It is our hope and intent to offer enough possibilities to enable the beginner to start the writing process and to motivate the writer who may need a laundry list of other alternatives to pursue. The library profession needs practitioners who are skilled communicators and who are interested in information sharing. If you want to become part of that process, we hope this book will offer the techniques, opportunities, and the inspiration you are looking for.

Appendix

Sample Author Guidelines

Following are a few sample guidelines from several library publications. From examining these, you will see there is a great deal of consistency in requirements of authors.

american libraries

GUIDES FOR SUBMITTING MANUSCRIPTS

American Libraries is a national magazine published by the American Library Association for its 40,000 members. It is also available to institutions by subscription. It carries material of interest to librarians, educational media specialists, and information scientists at all levels. Not a scholarly journal, it provides independent coverage of news and major developments in and related to the library field. Among its departments are: an open "opinion" column; highlights of life in modern libraries; and a section of concise current information in all major areas of the field, from intellectual freedom to technology. In addition, from one to three articles may be published each month on topics of major importance or special timeliness. Emphasis is on masterly and original treatment of any topic concerning librarians. American Libraries is also the magazine of record for general activities of the American Library Association, and the major vehicle of communication among its members.

The following are guidelines for submitting articles:

Style: Informal, but sophisticated. Factual articles must be inviting
             and readable, with all statements backed by responsible research.
             The Chicago Manual of Style is used in styling articles for pub-
             lication, but academic paraphernalia should be reduced to a minimum.

Length: 600-2,500 words (2-10 typed pages, doublespaced).

Copies: One original typed, double space. An extra copy is appreciated.
             Dot-matrix type accepted only if dark and highly readable.

Payment: An honorarium of $50 to $250 is offered for most accepted articles,
             paid upon signing of author-publisher agreement.

Exclusive
Submission: It is assumed that no other publisher is or will be considering a manuscript submitted to <u>American</u> <u>Libraries</u> until that manuscript is returned or written permission is provided by the <u>American</u> <u>Libraries</u> editors.

Rights: Exclusive North American rights are retained until three months after publication, unless another arrangement is made in writing. <u>American</u> <u>Libraries</u> retains rights to have the published material reproduced, distributed, and sold in microfilm or electronic text.

Reprint
Policy: No reprints can be provided, but permission is usually granted for authors to reproduce their contributions as published in <u>AL</u>. Special arrangements may be necessary to reproduce illustrations. Others wishing to republish the text of an article are referred to the author for permission and, if any, fee. A reasonable number of copies are sent to each author.

Acknowledgement: Unsolicited manuscripts are acknowledged when received.

Reports: The editors endeavor to report on manuscripts within 3-8 weeks. Written reminders from the author after this period are welcome, and usually result in a prompt reply.

Publication
Date: On acceptance, an estimated date of publication is provided to the author. Usually manuscripts can be published no sooner than two months after receipt.

Return of
Manuscripts: All rejected manuscripts are returned. A stamped, self-addressed envelope should be provided.

Editing: On accepted manuscripts, the editors reserve the right to make minor editorial revisions, deletions, or additions that, in their opinion, support the author's intent. When changes are substantial, every effort is made to work with the author.

Galleys: Galleys are not provided to the author.

Other materials used:

Photographs: Black-and-white glossies taken in natural light are preferred for use with manuscripts or as picture stories. Outstanding color slides or prints are considered for possible use. Payment is negotiated.

Cartoons: Cartoons of the highest professional quality that relate to library interests and avoid librarian stereotypes will be considered. Payment: $30-$60

Illustrations: Illustrations are commissioned for certain articles and features.

Reprinted by permission of the American Library Association.

About *College &*
Research Libraries

SUBMITTING
MANUSCRIPTS

Manuscripts of articles are to be sent to the editor, Charles R. Martell, c/o The Library, 2000 Jed Smith Dr., California State University, Sacramento, CA 95819.

Instructions for Authors

In preparing articles to be submitted for publication in *College & Research Libraries,* please follow these procedures:

1. Submit original, unpublished articles only. Authors are responsible for the accuracy of the statements in their articles. If the paper has been presented at a conference, identify the conference by name and date in a cover letter.

2. Manuscripts are to be typewritten, double-spaced, and submitted in three copies. The title, name, and affiliation of the author, and an abstract of seventy-five to one hundred words should precede the text. Do not repeat this information elsewhere in the text. Manuscripts usually range in length from one thousand to five thousand words, although longer manuscripts are occasionally received.

3. Bibliographical references are to be consecutively numbered throughout the manuscript, and typewritten, double-spaced, on a separate sheet or sheets at the end of the article.

4. Consult *Webster's New Collegiate Dictionary,* (supported by Webster's *Third International*), for spelling and usage; prefer the first spelling if there is a choice. Verify the spelling and accuracy of names in an appropriate reference.

5. The *C&RL* journal follows *The Chicago Manual of Style,* 13th ed., rev. (Chicago: Univ. of Chicago Pr., 1982) as authority for capitalization, punctuation, quotations, tables, captions, and all matters of bibliographical style. Authors may consult recent issues of the journal for examples of the style.

6. In general follow the practices recommended by *The Chicago Manual of Style* with these exceptions: Cite journal articles according to: author's first name or initials, author's surname, title of article, title of journal volume: page references (issue date). For example:

1. John Gardner and Gladys Rowe, "Thinking Small in a Big Way," *College & Research Libraries* 40:533–38 (Nov. 1979).

For subsequent references to a previously cited work, the surname of the author(s), a shortened form of the title, and the page reference are enough. Do not use *op. cit.* or *loc. cit.* For example:

15. Gardner and Rowe, "Thinking Small," p.534.

If no other reference intervenes, use "Ibid." to take the place of the elements of the previous reference that apply. Do not underline "Ibid." Do underline or quote all titles in both references and bibliographies. Number items as 1., 2., etc., but do not use superscript numbers. Use p.726–30, not pp. 726–730- for citations to a book or journal when listing page numbers. Abbreviate volume as V.2 or 2v. However, it is not necessary to give total number of pages or volumes when a reference cites an entire work. VERIFY ALL CITATIONS CAREFULLY.

7. Submit all tables and illustrations at the end of the paper, each on a separate page. Indicate the desired placement in the text by adding an instruction in brackets, e.g., (Insert table 2). Provide a brief title for each illustration or table. Type all tables double-spaced and follow the examples in *The Chicago Manual of Style* in constructing the tables, omitting the vertical lines to indicate columns. Use tables sparingly.

8. Submit original, camera-ready art for illustrations, figures, and graphs. Please protect camera-ready copy when mailing your manuscript. All original, camera-ready art will be returned to the author(s) after publication.

SUBJECT CONTENT

College & Research Libraries includes articles in all fields of interest and concern to academic and research librarians—for example, library collections, their acquisition and organization; services to readers and bibliographic instruction; library organization and management; library buildings; library history. In its treatment of a subject, the manuscript may employ a number of different approaches, for example, a case study or a descriptive or historical narrative, an article expressing informed opinion on a matter of continuing interest, a report on the procedures and results of a controlled research project.

REVIEW OF MANUSCRIPTS

Manuscripts received are given an initial review by the editor, and those selected for further review are submitted to at least two readers, generally from members of the Editorial Board. Names of authors are removed from the manuscript, and thus author identification should be on the first page of the manuscript only. Insofar as possible, other items in the manuscript that identify the author (e.g., a bibliographical reference) are blocked out by the editor prior to submission for formal review.

When the review is completed, generally in six to eight weeks, the editor notifies the author. An author is not to submit a manuscript to another publication while it is under review by *College & Research Libraries.*

In their review the readers will direct their attention to the content and style of the manuscript, addressing such questions as the following: Does the manuscript make a substantially new contribution to the literature? As for the method employed, is it appropriate to the subject, and does the author demonstrate competence with it? Is the author then able to communicate findings clearly to an educated yet not necessarily specialized audience? Does the author demonstrate through a review of the literature and other developments how the research or opinions here presented relate to them?

PUBLICATION

If accepted for publication, the manuscript is generally published from six to nine months after acceptance (depending on the supply of accepted manuscripts). The manuscript will be edited to conform to the style of the journal, and the editor may offer recommendations to the author on changes to make.

Articles published in *College & Research Libraries* are copyrighted by the American Library Association, and subsequent inquiries for reprinting articles are referred to the ALA Office of Rights and Permissions. All material in the journal subject to copyright by the American Library Association may be photocopied for the noncommercial purpose of scientific or educational advancement.

LETTERS

Readers are invited to comment on articles in the journal through letters addressed to the editor. It is recommended that such communications be as short as possible and no longer than 200 words. All letters should be typewritten, double-spaced. A letter commenting on an article in the journal is shared with the author, and a response from the author may appear with the letter.

REVIEWS

College & Research Libraries includes reviews and listings of new publications of interest to academic and research librarians. Publishers are invited to send review copies of their publications as well as announcements to the editor (Charles R. Martell, c/o The Library, 2000 Jed Smith Dr., California State University, Sacramento, CA 95819).

Readers wishing to review books for the journal are invited to write to the editor indicating their special areas of interest and qualifications.

Reprinted by permission of *College & Research Libraries.*

INSTRUCTIONS TO AUTHORS

SCOPE. RQ is the official journal of the Reference and Adult Services Division of the American Library Association. The purpose of *RQ* is to disseminate materials of interest to reference librarians, bibliographers, adult services librarians, and others interested in user-oriented library services, and to serve as a vehicle of communication among the membership of RASD. The scope of the journal includes all aspects of library service to adults, and reference service at every age level and for all types of libraries. (Adopted by RASD Board, June 27, 1973.)

Please follow these procedures when preparing manuscripts to be submitted to *RQ.*

1. Submit only original, unpublished articles on subjects within *RQ*'s scope. Articles of four thousand to six thousand words are preferred.
2. Write the article in a grammatically correct, simple, readable style. Remember that the author is responsible for the accuracy of all statements in the article.
3. Give the article a brief title; if the title is not descriptive of content, add a brief subtitle. On a separate page give the title, the name(s) of the author(s), and the title and affiliation of each. If the paper has been presented at a conference (the proceedings of which will not be published), identify the conference by name and date on the cover page.
4. On a separate page, type the title and subtitle, followed by a brief abstract typed double-spaced. Do not identify the author(s) here or elsewhere in the manuscript.
5. Consult Merriam-Webster's *New Collegiate Dictionary,* 9th ed., supplemented by Webster's *Third International,* as the authority for spelling and usage; prefer the first spelling if there is a choice. Verify the spelling and accuracy of names in an appropriate reference; don't rely solely on your memory.
6. As the authority for punctuation, capitalization, abbreviations, etc., consult *The Chicago Manual of Style,* 13th ed., rev. and expanded (Chicago: Univ. of Chicago Pr., 1982). (Hereafter cited as *Manual.*)
7. Type the manuscript, double-spaced, on 8½-by-11-inch nonerasable paper. TYPE ALL QUOTED TEXT DOUBLE-SPACED.
8. Submit all citations on separate pages at the end of the paper. TYPE THE REFERENCES DOUBLE-SPACED.
9. Citations should be made in the following form:
   1. W. W. Greg, "What Is Bibliography?" in J. C. Maxwell, ed., *Collected Papers* (Oxford: Clarendon Pr., 1966), p.75–88.
   2. John E. Baird, Jr., "Sex Differences in Group Communication: A Review of Relevant Research," *Quarterly Journal of Speech* 62:179–92 (Apr. 1976).
   3. Ibid, p.180.
   4. Greg, "What Is Bibliography?" p.84. Other questions on style and preparation of copy can be answered by the *Manual.* VERIFY EACH CITATION CAREFULLY.
10. TABLES, FIGURES, ILLUSTRATIONS, PHOTOGRAPHS. Each table should be typed on a separate sheet, double-spaced, given an arabic number, and cited in the text. Each column in a table should have a heading. Vertical rules should not be used. Table footnotes and sources, if any, should be typed double-spaced

beneath the table. Supply all drawings and/or photographs for figures and illustrations. Each figure should be given an arabic number and a title and cited by number in the text. The figure number should be marked on each drawing and on the back of each photograph (in soft pencil), and the figure numbers and titles should be typed double-spaced on a separate sheet. Drawings should be original artwork done in black india ink on white paper. Photographs should be original black-and-white glossy prints. Never clip anything to a photograph. When selecting or preparing drawings or photographs, keep in mind that they should be large enough and clear enough to permit a reduction of one-half to one-third. Avoid referring to tables and figures in phrases such as "the following," "above," "below"; it may be impossible to place the tables or figures to correspond. Refer always to "table 2," "figure 6," etc.

11. EDITING. Articles are edited to improve the effectiveness of communication between author and reader. When extensive editing is necessary, the article will be returned to the author for correction and approval. A copyright agreement form will be sent to each author when the manuscript is accepted for publication. Authors will receive galley proofs of their articles. Questions from the typesetter may require immediate communication with the editor. Drawings and photographs will not appear in the galley proofs. Page proofs are not sent to authors.

12. Send the original and two photocopies of your manuscript to Kathleen M. Heim, Editor, *RQ*, School of Library and Information Science, Louisiana State University, Coates Hall, Room 267, Baton Rouge, LA 70803. Please include an addressed envelope, large enough and with sufficient postage, to return the manuscript to you after the editorial review.

RQ complies with the "Guidelines for Authors, Editors, and Publishers of Literature in the Library and Information Field," passed as Council 1982-83 Document no.38. Copies may be obtained by writing ALA Executive Office, 50 E. Huron St., Chicago, IL 60611.

Reprinted with permission of the American Library Association, Reference and Adult Services, *RQ*.

JOURNAL OF LIBRARY HISTORY

The *Journal of Library History* is edited at the Graduate School of Library and Information Science, The University of Texas at Austin, and is published quarterly by the University of Texas Press. All views or conclusions are those of the authors and not necessarily those of the editorial staff, the University of Texas Press, The University of Texas at Austin, or The University of Texas System. From its establishment in 1966 until 1976, the *Journal* was edited and published by the School of Library Science, Florida State University, Tallahassee.

The editor invites scholarly contributions for consideration by the editorial board and referees. Three copies of each manuscript and an abstract of no more than 150 words should be sent, accompanied by a self-addressed, manuscript-size envelope and return postage. Manuscripts and footnotes must conform with The *Chicago Manual of Style*, 13th edition. Manuscripts and footnotes must be double-spaced with footnotes gathered at the end, using style *A*.

Manuscripts and editorial correspondence: The Editor, *Journal of Library History*, Graduate School of Library and Information Science, The University of Texas at Austin, Box 7576, University Station, Austin, Texas 78712.

Subscriptions and business correspondence: *Journal of Library History*, University of Texas Press, Box 7819, Austin, Texas 78712.

Subscription Rates: Individuals, $18.00/year; Institutions, $24.00/year. Countries other than U.S., add $3.00 to each year's subscription. Single copy, $7.00.

JLH is indexed in *America: History and Life*; *Book Review Index*; *Bulletin des Bibliothèques de France*; *Information Science Abstracts*; *Journal of American History* (Organization of American Historians); *Historical Abstracts*; *Library and Information Science Abstracts*; *Library Literature*; *MLA International Bibliography*; *Social Sciences Citation Index*; *Recently Published Articles* (American Historical Association). Previous volumes are available in microfilm from University Microfilms, 300 North Zeeb Road, Ann Arbor, Michigan 48106.

The Journal of Library History (ISSN 0275-3650) is published quarterly in February, May, August, and November by the University of Texas Press, P.O. Box 7819, Austin, Texas 78712. The rates are $24.00 a year for institutions and $18.00 a year for individuals. Second class postage paid at Austin, Texas and at additional mailing offices. POSTMASTER: Send address changes to *The Journal of Library History*, University of Texas Press, P.O. Box 7819, Austin, Texas 78712.

INSTRUCTIONS TO AUTHORS

Editorial correspondence should be directed to the Editor, THE LIBRARY QUARTERLY, Graduate Library School, University of Chicago, 1100 E. 57th Street, Chicago, Illinois 60637.

Library Quarterly is edited according to the University of Chicago Manual of Style, 13th edition, revised (1982). All manuscripts must be double-spaced (text, references, footnotes, figure legends, etc.). Allow right- and left-hand margins of at least 1½ inches each.

The first page of the manuscript should have the title of the article and, on a separate line, the name(s) of the author(s). The second page of the manuscript should consist of an abstract of 100–150 words. The text of the article should start on the third page.

The references follow the text and should be typed on a separate page or pages (all double-spaced). They should be numbered consecutively and should correspond with the numbers in the text (do not start numbers anew on each page of text). Each citation should be typed in full and only once. Subsequent references to it in the text should make use of the same reference number. Do not use ibid., op. cit., or loc. cit. Reference numbers should be included in the text in brackets. The citation in the list of references at the end should give inclusive paging of the reference. Citation to a single page or pages within the text should indicate those pages with the reference number. For example, [13, p. 6] or [7, pp. 18–19]. Examples of style for references are as follows:

For a journal article: Authors' names (inverted); article title (in quotes); journal title in full (underlined); volume number; month and year of publication (in parentheses); page numbers of entire article. Example:

    1. Squire, James. "Student Reading and the High School Library." *School Libraries* 15 (May 1966): 15–23.

For a book title: Authors' names (inverted); book title (underlined); city of publication; publisher; year. Example:

    2. Crowley, Terence, and Childers, Thomas. *Information Service in Public Libraries: Two Studies*. Metuchen, N.J.: Scarecrow Press, 1971.

Chapter in edited book:

3. Clapham, Michael. "Printing." In *A History of Technology*, edited by Charles Singer et al. . Vol. 3. New York: Oxford University Press, 1957.

Dissertation or thesis:

4. Jones, John L. "The Availability of Books in Tahiti." Ph.D. dissertation, University of Chicago, 1970.

Footnotes (typed paragraph style) should be placed together on typed sheets following the references. They should be numbered in order and should correspond with the numbers in the text. In the text, footnote numbers should be shown as superscripts (i.e., slightly above the line). Examples:

[Text] . . . . in the study.[4]

[Footnote] . . 4. J. P. Jones, etc.

Footnotes are not necessary if only to refer to a work cited. In this case, the reference number should be placed in the text brackets. Example: . . . . in that study [1, pp. 8–14]. Footnotes are only necessary for further explanation of something within the text. A footnote may be included giving acknowledgments or information on grants received by the author, and it should be marked as footnote 1 (append a superscript 1 to the article title).

Each table should be on a separate sheet of paper following the footnotes. Each table should be numbered and should be referred to *in order* in the text.

Each illustration (figure) should be on a separate sheet of paper (originals or glossy photographs, no xeroxed copies), and should follow the tabular material. Legends for the illustrations should be typed in order on a sheet of paper which should accompany the illustrations. All illustrations should be referred to *in order* in the text as figure 1, figure 2, etc.

MANUSCRIPT ACCEPTANCE POLICY: While it is our policy to require the assignment of copyright on most journal articles, we do not usually request assignment of copyright for other contributions. Although the copyright to such a contribution may remain with the author, it is understood that, in return for publication, the journal has the nonexclusive right to publish the contribution and the continuing right, without limit, to include the contribution as part of any reprinting of the issue and/or volume of the journal in which the contribution first appeared by any means and in any format, including computer-assisted storage and readout, in which the issue and/or volume may be reproduced by the publisher or by its licensed agencies.

C&RL News guidelines for submission of articles or news items

A statement of purpose and content for College & Research Libraries News.

Purpose of *C&RL News*

College & Research Libraries News is the official news magazine of the Association of College & Research Libraries, a division of the American Library Association. Its purpose is to record significant activities of ACRL and to report news about academic and research libraries. As the official ACRL news magazine, *C&RL News* maintains a record of selected actions and policy statements of the association and publishes timely reports on the activities of ACRL and its sections, committees, discussion groups, councils, task forces, and chapters.

As a vehicle for communication among college and research libraries, *C&RL News* reports news items pertinent to academic and research librarianship, including information on bibliographic instruction, continuing education, appointments, acquisition of special collections, grants to libraries, new technology, and publications (brief notices).

The editor bears responsibility for the contents of each issue of *C&RL News*. Materials selected by the editor must be newsworthy, timely, and of practical value to people in the field. The editor has authority to decide what material is appropriate for publication, based on the following guidelines. The editor also reserves the right to make appropriate revisions in material selected for publication in order to standardize style or improve clarity (except official ACRL documents, president's letters, and similar material).

Statistical, theoretical, or research-oriented articles inappropriate for *C&RL News* will be forwarded to the editor of *College & Research Libraries* for review.

I. Length
Articles and columns should be no more than 3,000 words and no less than 500 words.

II. Style
C&RL News style is informal, but informative and precise.

III. Content
Materials selected should fall into one of the following categories:

a. Reports on a project, program, or research underway or recently completed dealing with a topic relevant to academic librarianship. Footnotes should be minimal and charts or tables avoided. These reports may be preliminary descriptions of programs or research to be published formally at a later date in library literature (*e.g.*, "Library In-struction within the Curriculum," December 1984).

b. Reports on a recent conference or workshop of interest to academic or research librarians (*e.g.*, "The Changing Role of Libraries in Higher Education: A Symposium at Northern Illinois," November 1984).

c. Reasoned and informed speculation or comment on a relevant topic, especially if solicited by the editor or an official ACRL group (*e.g.*, "Deacidification Dialogue," January 1985).

d. State-of-the-art reports on a relevant topic (*e.g.*, "A Closer Eye on Appraisals," February 1985).

e. Standards, guidelines, or recommendations of an ACRL committee or other official ACRL group (*e.g.*, "A Proposed Planning Process for ACRL," September 1984).

IV. Manuscript
Authors should submit two copies, double-spaced, following either the *Chicago Manual of Style* or Turabian.

The preferred typewriter elements are: Courier 10, Prestige Elite 12, or Letter Gothic 12.

The deadline for receipt of editorial copy is approximately the 26th of each month, for inclusion in the issue of the second month following.

V. Requests for Donations
C&RL News may occasionally print requests for the donation of books or materials to libraries, especially foreign libraries, which have suffered extensive loss through fire, hurricane, or other natural disaster. Other libraries soliciting contributions for other reasons will be referred to the rates for classified advertising in *C&RL News*.

Editor's Note: These guidelines were adopted by the C&RL News *Editorial Board at the Denver Midwinter Meeting on January 25, 1982.* ■■

Reprinted by permission of *College & Research Libraries News*.

INSTRUCTIONS FOR LIBRARY TRENDS AUTHORS

Most critical manuscript features for us are:

1. Double space everything, including references.

EXCEPTION: Generally, short, indented, single-spaced quotes
of a few lines only look awkward and interrupt the process
of reading along the page. Long quotes of more than 5 lines
of type should be indented and single-spaced. Another
option is double spacing and paraphrasing (no indention),
while giving credit to the original author(s).

2. Indent all paragraphs at least 5 spaces.

3. Use 1-1/4" margins on all sides on each page.

4. Make papers 20-25 pages long if in elite type (i.e., 12 characters per
inch) or 25-30 pages if in pica type (10 characters per inch). (References,
tables and other illustrative matter, and appendixes are not included in the
page count.)

5. Give author's position title, affiliation, address, and telephone number
(including area code) on the first page of the paper.

6. Use complete bibliographical references and do not abbreviate author
names, journal names, or book titles. (We make some exceptions--e.g., ALA,
ASIS, USGPO, JASIS.) Bibliographical data should include: author (no
initials unless that is the author's customary usage), title, and journal,
volume, month/season, year, pages or place, publisher, year, pages. See the
Chicago Manual of Style 13th ed. for further information.

7. Use a new citation each time reference is made to a previously cited
work.

8. If a passage is quoted, give the exact page or pages on which it
appears.

9. All illustrative matter (e.g., photos, tables, figures, diagrams,
charts) should be black-and-white, camera-ready copy, on separate sheets of
paper. Make a note in the text where illustrative matter should be
inserted--e.g., "(Insert TABLE 1 here.)"

10. Personal communications should include day, month, and year and name(s)
of the person(s) the author communicated with.

11. Archival papers and government documents references should follow the
Chicago Manual of Style (CSM) 13th ed. or the USGPO style manual can be
used for documents. Legal citations should use CSM or A Brief Form of
Citation (Harvard Law Review format).

AUTHORITIES FOR STYLE, USAGE, GRAMMAR, AND REFERENCES

Authorities to consult for usage, grammar, spelling, punctuation, and
style are: Chicago Manual of Style, Webster's Third New International
Dictionary, ALA Glossary, Fowler's Modern English Usage, Strunk and White's
The Elements of Style, and Bernstein's The Careful Writer.

DISCRETIONARY MATTERS

Generally, we prefer endnotes to footnotes. If it is a bibliographical reference, it usually can be numbered and included in the endnotes. Tables and other illustrative matter may require footnotes, however.

If the author has a qualification of the main discussion, it would be best included in the text; but if the author feels it to be tangential or of special interest only, it might be included in an endnote.

Most acronyms should be spelled out the first time they are used. Undoubtedly, some readers are new to the field; others are international readers unfamiliar with United States acronyms; and others are American readers unfamiliar with Canadian or British or international acronyms.

Except for references to major world cities--e.g., London, West Berlin, Paris, New York, Bangkok, Tokyo--most cities should be followed by state or province (U.S. or Canada) or country--e.g., London, Ontario; Paris, Illinois; Moscow, Idaho; Vancouver, Washington; Buchs, Switzerland.

If a questionnaire or a form was used in the research the author reports, such documents should be included in an appendix.

Ideally, a table should be complete in itself--i.e., the reader should not have to be familiar with the text to read and interpret the table. Also, the text should not recapitulate the contents of the table, but rather, text should interpret and amplify the table.

Usually, a table of additive or cumulative percentages should add up to 100 percent--i.e., not 99 or 101 or something else due to "rounding error."

Finally, directions for authors always look forbidding and many provisions seem picky. We cannot say often enough that we enjoy reading manuscripts and working with authors. When authors observe the style conventions, we need to spend less time on the mechanics of the manuscripts and can give our attention to the authors' words and ideas. We read for a living and we enjoy it. We read carefully and closely--more so than most will read the final copy--and there probably isn't a manuscript we haven't come to liking after our close association with it. Thanks for making our jobs interesting, and we promise you that we want our authors' work to look and read well. We are looking forward to reading your work: it truly is the best part of the job.

Sincerely,

UNIVERSITY OF ILLINOIS
GRADUATE SCHOOL OF LIBRARY
AND INFORMATION SCIENCE
PUBLICATIONS OFFICE EDITORS

Reprinted by permission of *Library Trends.*

Technicalities®

Guidelines for Authors

TECHNICALITIES would like to encourage you to join our family of contributors. If you read TECHNICALITIES regularly, you will recognize the kind of materials we prefer.

We are looking for:
- Article submissions
- Ideas for articles you'd like to read
- Comments and suggestions
- Letters to the Editor

We need creative and well-written articles for future issues. Articles which stir the readers' interest and imagination are the ones we like best. Articles concerning technical services (broadly interpreted), which are constructively critical, take a new approach to standard procedures, question long-standing practices, and provide insight into taboo library topics are all likely prospects.

Our standards for submission

Receiving articles written in a standard format saves our staff time and effort. We accept:
- Typed, double-spaced originals with 1½" margins all around. Please include a second copy of the manuscript.

- Enclose a stamped, self-addressed envelope if you'd like your original returned (assuming we are not able to publish it).
- Please label the envelope containing your article "Article Submission."
- Include your name, address, and title on the cover page underneath the title of the article.
- We like to use suitable photographs: authors as well as subject material where appropriate; these should be black and white glossies. Include a credit line if the photos are by someone other than the author.
- We reserve the right to edit all material.

If you are in doubt about our interest in your proposed article, please send us a query letter and we will respond promptly. Be sure to include the telephone number where you can be reached.

Editors: Jennifer Cargill and Brian Alley

Please submit articles and query letters to:

TECHNICALITIES
c/o Jennifer Cargill
5520 56th St., #1009
Lubbock, TX 79414

Topics of interest to the TECHNICALITIES reader

- Technical Services
- Information Science
- Technology
- Automation
- Information Handling
- Education of Librarians
- Career Alternatives
- New Techniques and Discoveries
- Networking
- Hazards in the Work Place
- Career Ladders
- Collection Development

  and many more

ORYX PRESS
2214 North Central at Encanto
Phoenix, Arizona 85004

Selected Resources

Alderson, William T. *Marking and Correcting Copy*. Nashville, TN: American Association for State and Local History, 1969.
Covers proofreader marks, preparation of photos, and style rules.

Andrews, Deborah, and Blickle, Margaret D. *Technical Writing: Principles and Forms*. 2d ed. New York: Macmillan Publishing Co., 1982.
Written as a textbook for technical writing courses. Covers style and techniques of organization and presentation. Covers various forms of writing such as abstracts, proposals, reports, articles, and correspondence.

Arms, V. M. "The Computer and the Process of Composition." *Pipeline* 8 (1) (1976): 1–18.
Describes the use of word processors in a program at Drexel University.

Arth, Marvin, and Ashmore, Helen. *The Newsletter Editor's Desk Book*. 3d ed. Shawnee Mission, KS: Parkway Press, 1984.
Describes the gathering, writing, illustrating, editing, producing, and distributing of news via newsletters, magazines, and newspapers. This is a discussion of journalism principles as applied to special-audience periodicals.

Asimov, Isaac. "The Word Processor and I." *Popular Computing* 1 (4) (February 1982): 32–34.
Asimov's endorsement of writing with a word processor.

Atkinson, William. *The Writer's Tax and Recordkeeping Handbook*. Chicago: Contemporary Books, 1983.
Covers legal deductions, depreciations, etc., associated with writing.

"Avoiding Handicapped Stereotypes: Guidelines for Writers, Editors, and Book Reviewers." *Interracial Books for Children Bulletin* 8 (6/7) (1977): 9.

Baker, Samm Sinclair. "Writing Proposals That Get Book Contracts." *The Writer* 95 (March 1982): 7–11.
Discusses routines tested and used by a successful nonfiction writer.

Balkin, Richard. *A Writer's Guide to Book Publishing*. New York: Hawthorn Books, 1977.
Includes a number of valuable tips on approaching a publisher, preparing a proposal, negotiating a contract, marketing, and self-publishing. Also provides a sample proposal, a sample contract, and an example of a reader's report.

Bates, Marcia. "Rigorous Systematic Bibliography." *RQ* 16 (Fall 1976): 7–26.

Provides helpful descriptions of types of bibliographies and specific principles of systematic bibliography compilation.

Bates, Peter. "How to Turn Your Writing into Communication." *Personal Computing* 8 (October 1984): 84–93.
Discusses writing using word processing.

Beach, Mark. *Editing Your Newsletter: A Guide to Writing, Design, and Production Editing.* Portland, OR: Coast to Coast Books, 1980.
Provides information on newsletter production covering goal setting, acquiring content, production (from typing to final product), distribution, and scheduling.

Beach, Richard. *Writing about Ourselves and Others.* Urbana, IL: ERIC and National Council of Teachers of English, 1977.
Offers tips on interviewing, writing drafts, and choosing topics.

Bean, J. C. "Computerized Word-Processing as an Aid to Revision." *College Composition and Communication* 34 (May 1983): 146–48.
Advocates using word processing, specifically because of ease of revision.

Beedon, Laurel, and Heinmiller, Joseph. *Writing for Education Journals.* Bloomington, IN: Phi Delta Kappa Educational Foundation, 1979.
Includes bibliography of education journals.

Belkin, Gary S. *Getting Published; A Guide for Businesspeople and Other Professionals.* New York: John Wiley and Sons, 1984.
A good general guide covering everything from budgeting time to using a word processor, to preparing a manuscript.

Bodian, Nat G. *Copywriter's Handbook.* Philadelphia, PA: ISI Press, 1984.
A guide to copyediting skills.

Bowman, Mary Ann, comp. *Library and Information Science Journals and Serials: An Analytical Guide.* Westport, CT: Greenwood Press, 1985.
Annotated, evaluative guide to periodical literature in library and information science.

Brady, John. *The Craft of Interviewing.* Cincinnati, OH: Writer's Digest Books, 1976.
Interviewing is often a difficult task; Brady's book offers dozens of tips and suggestions for successful interviewing.

Brogan, John A. *Clear Technical Writing.* New York: McGraw-Hill, 1973.
Outlines a programmed learning approach to technical writing that demonstrates how to improve writing and use proper structure.

Brookes, B. C. "Jesse Shera and the Theory of Bibliography." *Journal of Librarianship* 5 (October 1973): 233–45, 258.

Bruhaugh, William, ed. *The Writer's Resource Guide.* 2d ed. Cincinnati, OH: Writer's Digest, 1983.
Designed for freelance writers, this is a listing of more than 2,000 sources of information on just about any topic, even libraries.

Brunner, Ingrid; Mathes, J. C.; and Stevenson, Dwight W. *The Technician as Writer: Preparing Technical Reports.* Indianapolis, IN: Bobbs-Merrill, 1980.
Gives valuable information for those who must write a lot of on-the-job reports.

Bryer, Jackson R. "From Second-Class Citizenship to Respectability: The Odyssey of an Enumerative Bibliographer." *Literary Research Newsletter* 3 (1978): 55–61.
Details, through the autobiographical musings of an enumerative bibliographer, some insights into the development of this type of bibliography as recognized scholarly research.

Butcher, Judith. *Typescripts, Proofs and Indexes.* New York: Cambridge University Press, 1980.
This short (only 32 pages) guide gives information on creating accurate, consistent typescript for the publisher, typesetter, and eventual reader; also contains helpful information on correcting proofs.

Calder, Julian, and Garrett, John. *The 35mm Photographer's Handbook.* New York: Crown, 1983.
Gives truly useful information for the beginner or pro. If you want to supplement your articles with photographs, this is the handbook for you. If there is a single photography manual for writers, this is it.

Callanan, Joseph A. *Communicating: How to Organize Meetings and Presentations.* New York: Franklin Watts, 1984.
Discusses small and large meetings; gives practical information on organizing as well as being a participant.

Cappon, Rene J. *The Associated Press Guide to Good Writing.* Reading, MA: Addison-Wesley, 1982.
Offers a wide variety of examples of usage, language, tone, and other elements of writing. Aimed at the practicing journalist, it offers a wealth of applications for editors and writers in other areas as well.

Challis, A. James, and Alley, Brian. "Can You Hear Me at the Back of the Room?" *Technicalities,* 2 (July 1982): 12–15.
Gives advice on using audiovisual aids in presentations.

Colaianne, A. J. "The Aims and Methods of Annotated Bibliography." *Scholarly Publishing.* 11 (July 1980): 321–31.
Gives advice on the compilation of annotated bibliographies.

Crump, Spencer. *The Stylebook for Newswriting: A Manual for Newspapers, Magazines, and Radio/TV.* Corona del Mar, CA: Trans-Anglo Publishing Co., 1979.

Davis, Cullom; Back, Kathryn; and MacLean, Kay. *Oral History: From Tape to Type.* Chicago, IL: American Library Association, 1977.
Covers, among a variety of oral history topics, interviewing, transcribing, and editing in some detail; a good sourcebook for the beginning interviewer in search of techniques and guidance.

Day, Robert A. *How to Write and Publish a Scientific Paper.* 2d ed. Philadelphia, PA: ISI Press, 1983.
Termed a "writing cookbook," this is one of the best of the books on writing for a specific audience. Defines a scientific paper and gives advice on the title, listing the authors and their addresses, preparing the

abstract and introduction, and other tips on manuscript preparation. A helpful book for nonscience writers also.

Dodds, Robert H. *Writing for Technical and Business Magazines.* New York: John Wiley and Sons, 1969.
Discusses subject and audience, placing your article, editing, and provides appendices with rules on the mechanics of writing.

Evans, Martha M. "Bibliographic Control of Large Quantities of Research Materials." *RQ* 23 (Summer 1983): 393–99.
Offers helpful advice and practical knowledge gleaned by the author in the course of compiling an annotated bibliography.

Felt, Thomas E. *Researching, Writing, and Publishing Local History.* Nashville, TN: American Association for State and Local History, 1976.
Although subject specific, provides helpful information on researching, writing historical articles, and publishing one's own work.

Fisher, Margaret B., and Smith, Margaret Ruth. *Writing as a Professional Activity.* Washington, DC: National Association for Women Deans, Administrators, and Counselors, 1976.
Based on a series of writing workshops. Covers developing your own style and writing scholarly articles and books, including textbooks. Slanted toward academic publishing needs.

Fluegelman, Andrew, and Hewes, Jeremy Joan. *Writing in the Computer Age.* Garden City, NY: Anchor Press, 1983.
Emphasizes the use of word processing for writing.

Franklin, Karen. *You Name It! Helpful Hints for Editors of Canadian Journals, Reports, Newspapers, and Other Serial Publications.* Ottawa, ON Canada: National Library of Canada, 1984.
A bilingual editorial guide to Canadian publications.

Glenn, Peggy. *Publicity for Books and Authors.* Huntington Beach, CA: Ames-Allen, 1985.
Your success as a writer may depend to a large extent on how skillful you are at promoting yourself as an author and how well you promote your book. Glenn covers every aspect of promotion in this large-format, how-to book that appeals to every level of sophistication with special emphasis on the beginner.

Graves, Harold F., and Hoffman, Lyne S. S. *Report Writing.* 4th ed. Englewood Cliffs, NJ: Prentice-Hall, 1965.
Although primarily a text for writing business reports, does provide helpful guidance to acquiring basic skills.

Green, Lee. *101 Ways to Use the Overhead Projector.* Littleton, CO: Libraries Unlimited, 1982.
Gives advice to relieve anxiety in using a projector.

Guidelines for the Preparation of a Bibliography. Chicago: ALA, 1982.
The ALA-approved evaluation and compilation guidelines.

Harmon, Robert B. *Elements of a Bibliography: A Simplified Approach.* Metuchen, NJ: Scarecrow Press, 1981.
Discusses what should be considered in bibliography compilation.

Hewes, Jeremy Joan. "The Write Stuff." *PC World.* 2 (1) (January 1984): 168–72.
Lists routines and provides tips for writing, using a word processor.

Hill, Mary, and Cochran, Wendell. *Into Print: A Practical Guide to Writing, Illustrating, and Publishing.* Los Altos, CA: William Kaufman, Inc., 1977.
Gives easy-to-follow instructions for preparing a manuscript and locating or even becoming a publisher.

Holley, Frederick S., comp. *The Los Angeles Times Style Book: A Manual For Writers, Editors, Journalists and Students.* New York: New American Library, 1981.
Provides information for quick consultation whenever style and usage problems arise. The alphabetical arrangement of words and topics make it easy to use and a most practical addition to your desk reference collection.

Howell, John Bruce. *Style Manuals of the English-Speaking World: A Guide.* Phoenix, AZ: Oryx Press, 1983.
Lists annotated bibliography entries of style manuals, arranged by category for which the style manuals are or have been used. Covers manuals published from 1970 to 1983.

Katz, Sidney B.; Kapes, Jerome T.; and Zirkel, Percy A. *Resources for Writing for Publication in Education.* New York: Teachers College Press, Teachers College, Columbia University, 1980.
Gives guidance to publishing in the education field.

Kernaghan, Eileen. *The Upper Left Hand Corner: A Writer's Guide to the Northwest.* Seattle, WA: Madrona Pubs., Inc., 1977.
Presents a regional slant. Although aimed at the freelance writer, it has lots of good advice on tax preparation, contracts, query letters, proposals, and copyright.

Kett, Merriellyn, and Underwood, Virginia. *How to Avoid Sexism: A Guide for Writers, Editors, and Publishers.* Chicago: Lawrence Ragan Communications, 1978.
Discusses forms of address, sex roles, and stereotyping. Includes options and alternatives for modern writers.

Koslov, Marcia J. "Competency, Conduct and Conference: How to Be Effective at Meetings." In *Women and Library Management: Theories, Skills and Values,* edited by Darlene E. Weingand, pp.55–70. Ann Arbor, MI: Pierian Press, 1982.
How to conduct meetings effectively.

Kubis, Pat, and Howland, Bob. *Writing Fiction, Nonfiction, and How to Publish.* Reston, VA: Reston Publishing, 1985.
Tells how to write and then how to get it published. Practical approach with sound guidance.

Kurtz, David L., and Spitz, A. Edward. *An Academic Writer's Guide to Publishing in Business and Economic Journals.* 2d ed. Ypsilanti, MI: Eastern Michigan University, Bureau of Business Services and Research, 1974.
Lists business periodicals for potential authors. Includes publication requirements.

Larsen, Michael. *How to Write a Book Proposal.* Cincinnati, OH: Writer's Digest, 1985.
A thoroughly useful guide to proposal writing that is a "must" purchase for any serious writer.

Larson, Virginia. *How to Write a Winning Proposal.* Van Nuys, CA: Creative Book Co., 1976.
Tells how to put together an effective proposal for writing projects.

Lewis, Phillip V., and Baker, William H. *Business Report Writing.* Columbus, OH: Grid, 1978.
Discusses, in textbook form, business report writing; includes exercises.

Linton, Marigold. *A Simplified Style Manual: For the Preparation of Journal Articles in Psychology, Social Sciences, Education and Literature.* New York: Appleton-Century-Crofts, 1976.
A guide to publishing in these fields.

Lord, Robert. *Running Conventions, Conferences, and Meetings.* Amacon, 1981.
Discusses how to plan small to large meetings and the pitfalls to anticipate.

McWilliams, Peter. *The Word Processing Book: A Short Course in Computer Literacy.* Los Angeles: Prelude Press, 1982.
Describes what word processors are, how they're used, and how to select and purchase one. Includes discussion of brands in existence, which may be of limited use due to the outdated publication date.

Melin, Nancy Jean. "Publishing—How Does It Work? The Journal Literature." In *Women and Library Management: Theories, Skills and Values,* edited by Darlene E. Weingand., pp. 71–75. Ann Arbor, MI: Pierian Press, 1982.
Tells what periodicals commission articles and gives advice on where to send articles.

Miller, Casey, and Swift, Kate. *The Handbook of Nonsexist Writing.* New York: Lippincott and Crowell, 1980.
Uses examples to aid writers, editors, and speakers in conveying ideas clearly and concisely without being sexist.

Mullins, Carolyn J. *A Guide to Writing and Publishing in the Social and Behavioral Sciences.* New York: Wiley-Interscience, 1977.
Discusses writing drafts, revising, manuscript preparation, etc.

Nancarrow, Paula Reed, et al., comps. *Word Processors and the Writing Process: An Annotated Bibliography.* Westport, CT: Greenwood Press, 1984.
Describes publications that discuss using word processors in the writing process.

Payne, Thomas E. *Guide for Authors: Manuscript, Proof and Illustration.* 2d ed. Springfield, IL: C. C. Thomas, 1980.
Gives advice on preparing manuscripts and copyediting and illustrating them.

Polking, Kirk, and Meranus, Leonard S. *Law and the Writer.* Cincinnati, OH: Writer's Digest, 1978.
Tells how to recognize and avoid legal problems. Includes the 1978 copyright law.

Polking, Kirk; Chimsky, Jean; and Adkins, Rose. *The Beginning Writer's Answer Book.* Rev. ed. Cincinnati, OH: Writer's Digest, 1978.

Gives more than 500 questions—and the answers from *Writer's Digest* editors. Arranged by categories. Includes definitions of terms, tips on getting started, legal aspects, and common procedures.

Porter, Ray E. *The Writer's Manual.* Palm Springs, CA: Etc. Publications, 1977.
Provides a vast array of information on all aspects of writing compiled from dozens of contributors.

Pournelle, J. "Writing with a Microcomputer." *onComputing* 1 (1) (1979): 12–14, 16–19.
Learning how to write with a computer.

Powell, Walter W. *Getting into Print: The Decision-Making Process in Scholarly Publishing.* Chicago: University of Chicago Press, 1985.
An interesting and often enlightening study of how scholarly publishing houses determine what they will publish. Summarizes scholarly editorial work, including acquiring manuscripts, contracting for a book, and evaluating manuscripts (and using outside reviewers).

Rettig, James. "Reviewing the Reference Reviews." *Reference Services Review.* 9 (October/December 1981): 85–102.
Gives a description of procedures and policies followed by key review publications at the time of publication of this article.

Richardson, John V. "Readability and Readership of Journals in Library Science." *The Journal of Academic Librarianship* 3 (March 1977): 20–22.
Analyzes the readability of library professional periodicals.

Robinson, A. M. Lewin. *Systematic Bibliography: A Practical Guide to the Work of Compilation.* 3d rev. ed. Hamden, CT: Linnet Books, 1971.
Provides a definition of systematic bibliography and advice on how to approach compilation of them.

Shera, Jesse H., and Egan, Margaret E. "Foundations of a Theory of Bibliography." In Jesse H. Shera, *Libraries and the Organization of Knowledge,* by Jesse H. Shera, pp. 18–33. Hamden, CT: Archon Books, 1965.

Sides, Charles H. *How to Write Papers and Reports about Computer Technology.* Philadelphia, PA: ISI Press, 1984.

Snyder, Elayne. "The Best Little Meetings in the Company." *Working Woman* 9 (7) (July 1984): 51–55.
Gives tips on running meetings so they won't be time-wasters.

Steiner, Dale R. *Historical Journals: A Handbook for Writers and Reviewers.* Santa Barbara, CA: ABC-Clio, 1981.
Provides specific information on practices of different journals.

Stevens, Norman. "Writing for Publication." *Collection Management* 3 (Spring 1979): 21–29.

Stevens, Norman, ed. *Essays from the New England Academic Librarians' Writing Seminar.* Metuchen, NJ: Scarecrow Press, 1980.
A compilation of essays from a seminar where librarians critiqued their essays.

Stevens, Norman, and Stevens, Nora B. *Author's Guide to Journals in Library and Information Science.* New York: Haworth Press, 1982.
Lists periodicals in the library and information science field and indicates the type of articles each publishes.

Stratton, John, and Stratton, Dorothy. *Magic Writing: A Writer's Guide to Word Processing.* New York: New American Library, 1984.
Covers everything from buying on a budget to managing a spelling checker. This excellent guide is loaded with helpful hints and dozens of useful illustrations. No one learning word processing should be without a copy.

Strunk, William, Jr. and White, E. B. *The Elements of Style.* 3d ed. New York: Macmillan, 1979.
White revised Strunk's classic work. Includes elementary rules of usage, principles of composition, misused expressions, and comments on style.

Ullmann, John, and Honeyman, Steve, eds. *The Reporter's Handbook: An Investigator's Guide to Documents and Techniques.* New York: St. Martin's Press, 1983.
Covers sources and strategies for reporting in the public sector. Although intended primarily for investigative journalists, the book provides a variety of approaches to dealing with individuals and organizations in researching information of all kinds.

Van Leunen, Marie-Claire. *A Handbook for Scholars.* New York: Knopf, 1979.
Discusses scholarly writing. A good source for locating solutions to special writing problems. This book has received both favorable and unfavorable commentary from the scholarly community since some of the concepts related in the text are nontraditional.

Van Til, William. *Writing for Professional Publication.* Boston: Allyn and Bacon, 1981.
Loaded with ideas and examples for writers.

Werner, L. "Word Processing." *Popular Electronics* 19 (August 1981): 29–36.
Discusses different types of word processing hardware.

Wilson, Patrick. *Two Kinds of Power: An Essay on Bibliographical Control.* Berkeley: CA: University of California Press, 1968.

Writer's Market. Cincinnati, OH: Writer's Digest Books.
Revised and published yearly. Guide to types of writing; provides listing of publications and publishers to approach.

The Writing Business: A Poets and Writers Handbook. Wainscott, NY: Pushcart Press, 1985.
Describes the writing process, manuscript preparation, signing contracts, working with editors, and other topics.

Wyer, Mary. "Publishing—How does It Work? (Or, They Don't Call It "Submission" for Nothing)." In *Women and Library Management: Theories, Skills and Values,* edited by Darlene E. Weingand, pp. 77–80. Ann Arbor, MI: Pierian Press, 1982.
Gives advice on which approaches to use in contacting publishers.

Zinsser, William. *On Writing Well.* 2d ed. New York: Harper and Row, 1980.
   If you like to write, you'll enjoy this excellent book, dedicated to perfecting the craft. Tells how to express yourself effectively. Regarded as a classic.

————. *Writing with a Word Processor.* New York: Harper Colophon, 1983.
   Gives hints on writing using word processors.

Index

Compiled by Linda Webster